COCKBURN IN

Ivor
Montagu
Writes . . .
(See Page 4)

DAILY WORKER

WORKERS OF ALL LANDS UNITE

Sports
Round
About
(See Page 6)

No. 2301   REGISTERED AT THE G.P.O. AS A NEWSPAPER   THURSDAY, JUNE 3, 1937   One Penny

DURANGO! GUERNICA! ALMERIA!

LABOUR MUST CALL HALT TO NAZI MURDERERS

DIPLOMATIC CONVERSATIONS, IT WAS COOLLY ANNOUNCED YESTERDAY, ARE BEING CONDUCTED "WITH THE OBJECT OF EVOLVING A SCHEME WHICH WILL PREVENT A RECURRENCE OF SUCH EPISODES AS THE BOMBING OF THE DEUTSCHLAND."

While these were in process, the British Government, which did its best to hold up the arrival of the Basque children, which lifted no finger when Nazi planes massacred women, children and peaceful citizens of Guernica, Durango and other defenceless Basque towns, rushed four British Army nurses in two Army seaplanes non-stop from Calshot, Southampton, to Gibraltar.   For what?   To nurse the Nazi seamen, wounded when, in reply to the unprovoked aggression of the Deutschland, two Spanish Government planes bombed that vessel!

Not a word of protest in the Government-controlled Press!   Not a word even of concern for the victims of shattered Almeria!   But exposing itself finally and utterly in the eyes of the whole world, the British Government swings all the forces at its disposal, all its diplomacy, behind the murderers of Almeria and Guernica, and caps this by spending British public money in sending aid to the Nazi crews and never a penny on the victims of these Fascist barbarians.

IT IS ENOUGH!   LET LABOUR, WITH UNHESITATING DECISION AND UNBREAKABLE UNITY, ACT NOW TO LET THESE ACCESSORIES TO MURDER KNOW THAT THE BRITISH PEOPLE WILL NOT TOLERATE THIS ENORMITY.

Dogs Howl In Empty Almeria, People Hide In Caves—Nazis Came

FROM FRANK PITCAIRN

VALENCIA, Wednesday.

LAST night I stood at a window in Almeria and listened. Absolute silence except for first one and then another dog. The dogs ran about the streets looking for food.

Madrid and Valencia are silent at night, but that is a different sort of silence. By an incident of small magnitude you are aware of hundreds of thousands of people all around you, you can hear them breathing. Almeria at night is dead. Sixty-five thousand people lived there before the war. Tonight there are not much more than a thousand in the whole city.

The Nazis have driven them out.

Above the city you can see the ancient Roman ruins, and you begin to understand what the Romans felt like when the barbarians came.

Supposing this week a wandering attack in the New Forest or the Downs, looking for a comfortable case to settle down in; thousands of others coming into town every morning early and leaving again at night—for four the Nazis should come again.

There is still a certain amount of work for civilians to do in Almeria. For instance, the first man I saw at work in the morning was the coffin-maker, who is busy already and expects to be busier still. As this, you wonder, really the state of things to come?

The big construction works in the city is something that looks as though it were going to be an underground railway. It turned out to be a vast system of subterranean bombproof refuges and passages but the civilians from the environs when they are not the principals of multitudes who are here peaceful.

During the daytime you can in many parts of the town have the illusion that nothing at all has happened. You would expect to see something "normal" somewhere. On the contrary, things look what we have labelled to be calling "normal."

For business there is the façade of the Gran Hotel. It looks all right. Nothing has happened there from within. Then you step inside and see the pile of dusty lines—the ferns of a place that has been shattered by a German shell and the roar that of having down so attempts to remove eleven or fifth and clatter.

Over there is the civilian hospital. It appears untouched. You go upstairs and find that where the back of the hospital is. The next higher up, the roof of the Sebastian Church, the church of St. Sebastian, scheduled by the Nazis for this series of air city, hit the street and beyond.

Two feet in the air above the street, carrying shrapnel up to the famous widow reach. They also found shrapnel shells into the other street. This was a good idea of the German since might who raised shells go streaming methodically out from the homes had a good

chance of being killed by shrapnel in the open streets.

I met a young doctor, a very medical person, looking. The an average young doctor of a large provincial town. His name is Louis Graffe. What happened to the Graffe family is typical of what happened to people in Almeria when the Nazis ran in the battleship.

Louis Graffe himself was working at the military hospital. A shell fell in the garden. All over the town great clouds of smoke arose and black mounds of red brick dust began to appear on the roads once the tiles that a cloud.

A ambulance was driving through the fire of a shrill begin dashing up with wounded. Then when they started to operate they found the water, electricity and gas had all been cut off by the shelling.

Meantime Graffe's old mother and father had been taken to their homes on the second floor of a block. A little later an enemy round fell behind that block in the street.

The children were closed. They were screaming in the darkness by the whistling of the shells and the crashing all around. They dared not open the shutters to see what was beyond.

Like thousands of other families in Almeria that morning they crowded together in a corner of the room upsetting, so people do in such a situation, that the corner would somehow be safer than any other part of the house.

(Continued on Page Eight)

U-BOATS AGAINST SPAIN

BERLIN, Wednesday.

FOUR German submarines left yesterday for Spanish waters.

It is learned that the submarines are the U 28, U 35, U 34 and U 35.

Each is of 500 tons, carries a crew of 35 and is armed with one 3.5-inch gun, one machine-gun and five torpedo tubes.—Exchange Telegraph.

EXECUTIVE CALLED "INEPT"

We Gave The Derby Winner

By THE SPORTS EDITOR

CAYTON, the Daily Worker racing correspondent, again came up trumps yesterday, when Mid-Day Sun, his tip for the Derby stakes, flashed past the post as the winner at 100 to 7. This triumph is all the more significant since we were the only national daily newspaper to select the winner.

There were no ifs and buts about Cayton's selection. He gave it, fully confident of the colt's ability to win.

He supplied his readers when Wakefield, his big selection, romped home at 1 to 3, the gelding in Tate stakes for the day.

From another tender his atmosphere even bigger than usual, it being commented that even Stable people were on the Epsom Downs when the Derby was run.

At time o'clock the great trek had begun. Cars of all descriptions could be seen wending their way towards Epsom, while many thousands of people were on foot.

Late starters from London had the usual difficulty in getting through to the course. From the outskirts and through the Kingdom 6-pass the traffic blockage was the greatest ever experienced.

SAME OLD DERBY

As usual, it was a curious mixture here, banks of musicians and individuals using their best to

amuse the crowd. People, however, mainly thronged in the huge fairground, where a terrible amount of forces and confusion, added to the din of bumorators "governments" showing their readiness to make anybody's fortune by buying their tips.

This was the workers' day out with a vengeance. Those who could not see anything of the race were spending their time of occasional rides, merry-go-rounds, swing-boats, and the various palaces of variety.

When time money had proceeded home the traffic congestion passed even worse than before its race, and it was many hours before Epsom emptied.

BIG PRICE CUT IN SOVIET UNION

(From Our Own Correspondent)

MOSCOW, Wednesday.

THE decision of the Soviet Government to reduce the prices of consumption goods by between 5 and 10 per cent., came into operation yesterday. The price of articles of secondary importance will be lowered on July 1.

The present reduction constitutes another link in the consistent policy of the Soviet Government which permits the steadily raising the material welfare of the masses in the towns and the countryside of the Socialist Fatherland, in contrast with the diminishing importance to the standard of living of the people in the capitalist countries.

GREAT SAVINGS

The fulfilment of the Second Five-Year Plan before the scheduled date means an accumulation of additional material resources which make possible the present price reductions.

In 1935 since the Soviet people saved 1,200,000,000 roubles as the result of price reductions. This should be added 2,000,000,000 roubles which the people gained as a result of cuts in the collective farm markets. Last year the people saved 5,000,000,000 roubles through price cuts in Government and Co-operative trade prices.

Indication of the growing welfare of the people is the increased retail trade from 25.5 thousand million roubles in 1931 to 106 thousand million roubles in 1936.

Immediately the result of the Derby became known we had many telephones calls of congratulations. One East London worker tells us that the Daily Worker tip, the winner Mid-Day Sun, was given at East London meetings, and as a result of this selection many East London workers had "done themselves a bit of good."

In addition, many copies of the Daily Worker were sold on Wednesday morning on the paper's Derby selection.

Big Vote For New Policy

From Our Special Correspondent, FRED PATEMAN

SCARBOROUGH, Wednesday.

THERE was a sharp down and a close vote on a resolution from the London Division, which Mr. Little said the executive committee would regard as a vote of censure.

The resolution, defeated by 21 votes to 14, with five dissentients, had already been the subject of a hot-fought debate yesterday, when it was turned on Tuesday to line of strong opposition from the executive council.

The terms of the resolution were: "That this National Committee views with alarm and indignation the ineptitude of the executive council to take advantage of the present situation and the membership towards a solution of long-standing grievances. We view with apprehension the apparent indifference of the executive council to make demonstration of the National Committee from time to time."

LACK OF ENTHUSIASM

"We call the attention of executive council to the progress advance endorsed at the last term accepted, and the Gentleman's Agreement observed by units, and the absence of any effort to make the membership on the question or the renovation of the club, etc.

"Further, this National Committee shall adequate the introduction of the agenda for a period of six months for a more expeditious from the Executive Council under progress made in carrying out decisions arrived at."

The whole basis of the resolution was the feeling that greater speed is needed in obtaining a concession of the employers' demand on wages, hours and conditions, said Mr. J. B. Longworth, moving the resolution, said the London District felt that talk had gone on long enough. The resolution was passed the employers would usually change their attitude.

Mr. T. Tomalin, also of London, declared that on organisation ended only get somewhere if it was voiced and out to get somewhere.

Mr. F. Silvers, Glasgow, said the knives for unofficial strikes on the slowing with the local of the executive council to somehow seriously the workers' grievances.

Mr. E. C. Lyons, replying for the Executive Council, said he contended any charge being made which was not based on fact. He gave details of what the Executive Council had done on each of the points raised in the resolution, but had to admit that provisions for the avoidance of disputes procured by inevitable mechanism, which operates under the Joint Industrial Council.

Mr. Longworth, replying to the debate, stressed that the purpose of the resolution was to get a move-on the speeding up of a settlement. He did not wish to make it a vote-of-censure.

Finally, he recalled the very successful exertions out of the London ship repair engineers, which, showed what could be done by action as opposed to talk.

The big vote against the policy of the Executive Council was a symptom which may be taken as reflecting the feeling for action among the workers in the industry.

Tonight—Rally To The House

SUMMONED at 24 hours' notice, a mighty demonstration took place in Hyde Park on Tuesday night to protest with vigour and passion against the German outrage at Almeria.   The march to the German Embassy in London was such that it became in itself an important political action in reply to Hitler's latest example of Fascist frightfulness.   In it, too, the growing political influence of the Daily Worker was reflected.

To make protest even more forceful, through D. F. Springhall, the London District Committee of the Communist Party calls upon all London workers, all anti-Fascists and friends of peace, to present themselves at the House of Commons tonight at 8.45 prompt, and to exercise their right as citizens to express

their viewpoint in this hour of crisis to their Member of Parliament.

This action is to be followed on Sunday by an all-London march, starting at Hyde Park at 3 p.m.

Only those members of the Communist Party who are mentioned in the "What's On" column are excused from taking part.

In the name of humanity, in the cause of the defence of the Spanish women and children, in the interests of European peace, this call to action is sounded.

Let the response be worthy of London's best traditions in the noble cause of peace.

TWO INJURED IN LADDER FALL

Aaron Atherton, aged 60, of Grasmere Avenue, High Wyott, and his son, Samuel Atherton (31), were taken to hospital yesterday afternoon, after falling from a ladder at their home at Ealing.

COCKBURN IN SPAIN

Despatches From the Spanish Civil War

Edited by James Pettifer

LAWRENCE AND WISHART
LONDON

Lawrence and Wishart Limited
39 Museum Street
London WC1A 1LQ

First published 1986

Photoset in North Wales by
Derek Doyle & Associates, Mold, Clwyd.
Printed in Great Britain by
Oxford University Press

Contents

2   THE STRUGGLE FOR MADRID

3   FROM MÁLAGA TO THE FOREIGN OFFICE BAN

4   COCKBURN'S PASSPORT, THE POUM RISING, ALMERÍA

5   DEFEAT AND THE WIDER CRISIS

All items, except where indicated otherwise, are taken from the
Daily Worker.

Acknowledgements

We are grateful to the *Morning Star* for permission to reproduce the material from the *Daily Worker*, to Mrs Patricia Cockburn for permission to reproduce excerpts from *Reporter in Spain* and other material held in her copyright, and to the Marx Memorial Library for assistance with the frontispiece.

Chronology

1931

13 April   Fall of Spanish monarchy and declaration of Republic.

27 October   National Government, dominated by Conservatives, wins British General Election.

1933

30 January   Hitler becomes Chancellor in Germany.

1934

12 February   Dollfuss liquidates left-wing opposition in Austria.

October   Franco puts down miners' rising in Asturias with considerable brutality.

1935

August   Communist International launches Popular Front policy.

14 November   Conservatives win British General Election.

1936

16 February   Popular Front wins Spanish General Election.

7 March   Nazi troops seize demilitarised Rhineland.

3 May   Popular Front wins French General Election.

9 May   Fascist Italy annexes Abyssinia.

18 July   Army revolt against Spanish Popular Front government.

25 July   French government forbids arms sales to Republican Spain.

1 September   Franco declared head of state.

4 September   Largo Caballero becomes Prime Minister of Republican government; fall of Irún, Basque country cut off from France.

9 September   Non-Intervention Committee meets in London.

12 October   Formation of International Brigades.

6 November   Republican government leaves Madrid for Valencia.

8 November   XIth International Brigade in action in Madrid.

1937

9 January	British government threatens volunteers with Foreign Enlistment Act.
31 January	Formation of XVth International Brigade, including British Battalion.
6 February	Battle of Jarama begins.
8 February	Fall of Málaga.
26 April	Bombing of Guernica.
4 May	Uprising in Barcelona by POUM and anarchists.
18 May	Negrín replaces Caballero as Prime Minister.
31 May	Nazi naval bombardment of Almería.
19 June	Fall of Bilbao.
6 July	Brunete offensive begins.
21 October	Fall of Gijón and Asturias, north of Spain entirely in Nationalist hands.
15 December	Teruel offensive begins.

1938

20 February	Anthony Eden resigns as Foreign Secretary over British Appeasement of Fascist Italy and is replaced by Earl of Halifax.
9 March	Major Nationalist offensive in Aragon.
11 March	Nazi Germany invades Austria.
2 April	International Brigades base moves from Albacete to Barcelona.
15 April	Nationalists reach Mediterranean – Republic cut in two.
25 July	Ebro offensive begins.
21 September	Negrín announces withdrawal of International Brigades.
22 September	British Battalion fights its last battle in the Sierra del Lavall.
29 September	Chamberlain meets Hitler and Mussolini and signs Munich agreement.
29 October	International Brigades farewell parade in Barcelona.
7 December	British volunteers arrive back in London.

1939

26 January	Fall of Barcelona.
15 March	Nazi Germany invades Czechoslovakia.
28 March	Fall of Madrid, defeat of Republic.
1 September	Nazi Germany invades Poland.

Introduction

Shortly before Claud Cockburn's death in 1981, Graham Greene wrote of him:

> If I were asked who are the two greatest journalists of the twentieth century, my answer would be G.K. Chesterton and Claud Cockburn. Both are more than journalists: both produced at least one novel which will be rediscovered with delight, I believe, in every generation – *The Man who was Thursday* and *Ballantyne's Folly*. Both are manic characters, writing with what some sad fellows may find even an excess of high spirits. Perhaps Claud Cockburn will prove to have been more influential, for he discovered the influence that can be wielded by a mimeographed news-sheet.

In recent years this widely-acknowledged reputation has seemed more and more to rest on *The Week*, the duplicated news-sheet that Cockburn founded in 1933, which soon became famous for its exposure of the machinations of the Conservative government in the later years of the decade. More than anything else published at the time, *The Week* brought home to its subscribers the nature of Appeasement, and how a dominant section of the Conservative Party was assisting the foreign policy of the fascist dictators, and drew attention to the 'Cliveden Set' of wealthy pro-Hitler interests that existed at the time in British ruling circles.

But *The Week*, extraordinary though its influence was, was not a vehicle which a gifted journalist could use to the exclusion of all others. It was produced hurriedly, in conditions of exceptional material difficulty, from a tiny office in Victoria. It was very small, physically, perhaps only a fifth of the size of a current issue of *Private Eye*, and it had to be packed with factual information and news analysis. Space was at such a premium that stories in *The Week* were often reduced to a single sentence or paragraph.

Cockburn's connection with the *Daily Worker* had begun in September 1934 when Harry Pollitt, the General Secretary of the Communist Party, asked him to cover the Gresford mining disaster for the paper. He gives an account of the beginning of his contact in the second volume of his autobiography, *In Time of Trouble*:

> It was at about this time that Mr Pollitt, Secretary of the Communist Party of Great Britain, whom I had never met, was suddenly announced on the telephone – would I, he asked, take the next train, in twenty minutes or half an hour, and report a mine disaster at Gresford, North Wales. Why? Because he had a feeling that there was a lot more in it than met the eye. But why I in particular? Well, because, it seemed, Mr Pollitt – who was worrying at the time about what he believed to be a lack of 'reader appeal' in the *Daily Worker* – had been reading *The Week* and thought I might do a good job.

It seems clear that Pollitt saw the potential of Cockburn's writing talents for the *Daily Worker*, and over the next eighteen months or so he covered some big set-piece stories for the paper, particularly the events leading up to the election of the Popular Front government in France in 1936. But it was not very long before a situation arose that would give Cockburn particular scope for his journalistic talent. With the outbreak of the Spanish Civil War it was natural for the *Daily Worker*, poor as it was, to send a full-time correspondent. The struggle to defend the legally-elected left-wing government against the rebellious Nationalist generals aided by Hitler and Mussolini was seen as a central priority for Communist parties and the left in general. Volunteers were already leaving Britain and other countries to fight on the Republican side well before the formal decision of the Comintern to organise the formation of brigades of international volunteers later in 1936.

Apart from minor incidents on the fringes of the Empire, the ill-fated intervention against the Soviet Union in Archangel, and the war in Ireland in the early 1920s, Britain had been at peace since the end of the First World War, and the trade of war correspondent was a new one to Cockburn, as it was to nearly all the journalists and writers who were sent to Spain. As a *Times* journalist in Berlin and New York, he had been covering normal political and diplomatic activity, and much of his work on *The Week* was a continuation of that, in content if not in approach. *The Week* was almost exclusively concerned with the life of the ruling classes in the different European countries, and exposing inner machinations to a wider public, but they remained conspiracies that took place in drawing-rooms, in banks, in clubs and in officers' messes. The open spaces of the Spanish sierras, with hundreds of thousands of people involved in a life-or-death struggle for the preservation of democracy, were very different.

Spain, neutral in the First World War, had not hitherto been considered an important nation in a Europe that was still dominated by the traditional powers – Britain, France, Germany and Italy – whose status was in a large part determined by their colonial possessions. Although he had visited the country in 1934, and had seen the aftermath of the crushing of the Asturian miners' rising by a then little-known army officer named Francisco Franco y Bahamonde, there is no reason to suppose Cockburn had any specialised knowledge of the country before the Civil War started. In this he had much in common with most British people at the time, whatever their class or background, who in the days before mass-tourism probably thought little of Spain except that it was a backward, priest-ridden country that had at some time in the remote past produced something called the Spanish Armada. Historically, Britain's commercial and diplomatic relations with the Iberian peninsula had centred on Portugal rather than on Spain.

Cockburn's job, as *Daily Worker* special correspondent, was to fill in this gap in British public knowledge, as quickly as possible, and make clear that the officers' revolt had a much wider significance. The Communist Party leadership, as the main driving force behind the Spanish Aid committees that had sprung up, realised quite early on that one of the main problems in developing mass solidarity with the Republic was the general impression in Britain that Spain was, in the same way as Neville Chamberlain described Czechoslovakia, a 'far away country of which we know little'. Cockburn's job in Spain was not simply to report events in the war effectively, and to get the point of view of the Republican government across to the British people, but to bring the struggle in the country alive in such a way as it would catch their imagination and fire them to take action.

His first stint in the country started in mid-summer 1936, and covered the early days of Nationalist advance in the south, and the preparations for the defence of Madrid against the four main columns of the rebel army. It offered extraordinary opportunities to all the correspondents who were there, as he makes clear in his autobiography:

There was little time to attend thoroughly to the King business, because what we had now was the Spanish War.

A complacent ass who was, temporarily, Propaganda Minister of Catalonia, said to me: 'This is the most photogenic war anyone ever has seen.'

Considering that people were dying all around us – many of them having come to meet death with extreme heroism because they believed this to be the final battleground where, as in children's stories, the Good get to grips with the Bad – his remark was offensive. Indeed it indicated to any clear-sighted observer that the man thought we were probably going to lose, and was making jokes until he could make up his mind which way his cat would, or could, jump.

All the same, there was a streak of truth in what he so ineptly said.

That terrible war was also 'photogenic' in the widest sense of the word. Not just the press photographers turned up, everyone turned up who wanted to be in on the decisive thing of the century, the thing that was going to prove either that Democracy was going to stand up to the enemy there and then, or else that Democracy – it was the phrase people used at the time, and they believed in it – was going to take a terrible beating, and after that there would be a bigger and worse war.

The massacres and the battles and the subsequent massacres took place, too, in lovely surroundings.

He joined the Fifth Regiment that was being formed to defend the capital, as a private, and took part in the militia training programme. After this, he saw action during the first desperate days fighting when the Republican forces fought to halt the Nationalist advance from the south. His reportage during this period was unique in journalistic history, seeing, as it does, what he later described as the 'makeshift, ramshackle quality of the Spanish War' from the point of view of a rank-and-file soldier.

Back in London the main priority was to move the Labour Party and TUC from their inaction to a position of active practical support for the Republic. Cockburn returned to Britain for a speaking tour, the highlight of which was a mass meeting at Shoreditch Town Hall. After the tour, Pollitt, recognising the great impact that Cockburn's despatches were having, told him to stay in London and write a book about the war and its background, with the same general purpose as the *Daily Worker* articles. *Reporter in Spain* was written at great speed in the early autumn of 1936, and was on sale soon afterwards. Cockburn then returned to Spain and covered the autumn and winter battles to hold the line round the capital, and ventured further afield when the opportunity arose. This period of work culminated in the Battle of Jarama, in February 1937, when in the bitter struggle to stop the Nationalists cutting the Madrid to

Valencia road, the British Battalion suffered such severe losses that only 225 out of its original 600 members were left at the end of the day.

His contribution to developing the understanding of the struggle was, however, being recognised in other quarters as well. The Foreign Office, a stronghold of pro-Franco feeling, had withdrawn his visa, and it was only after delays and a Parliamentary campaign that he was able to get it back. This wasted a great deal of his time and energy in March 1937, a critical time in the war, and meant that Cockburn could not leave London.

By this stage, anyway, the character of the journalistic coverage that the *Daily Worker* followed had begun to change. People in Britain, well outside the ranks of the political left, had begun to realise more clearly what was at stake. The volunteers in the British Battalion were beginning to contribute their own material to the paper, and to other papers on the left. The heavy losses suffered by the British had led to a succession of obituary notices and tributes to the fallen in the *Daily Worker*. It must have seemed as if their actions could speak louder to the readers than any journalist's words, however gifted the writer. Although Cockburn remained in Spain for long periods in 1937, the amount of Spanish material printed declined considerably. Other correspondents were active for the paper, some of whom, like Peter Kerrigan, had originally been members of the British Battalion. It should also be noted that in the generally worsening international atmosphere, other crises were developing that inevitably made the left's concentration on Spain less exclusive as the war dragged on. As early as October 1937, a main feature article in the *Daily Worker* by John Strachey, ran under the headline 'Don't Forget Spain' – and this was when the war still had a long time to go. In January 1938, Bill Rust, later to be perhaps the most successful editor the paper ever had, became special correspondent in Spain, and Cockburn's despatches stopped. Harry Pollitt himself went back to Spain and wrote a series of articles from the front, Clem Atlee visited for the Labour Party and the gruesome last months passed into the hands of the political leaders.

Cockburn had formed a close personal relationship in Spain with Mikhail Koltsov, then the foreign editor of *Pravda* and at that time, in Cockburn's view, 'the confidant and mouthpiece and direct agent of Stalin in Spain'. Through this relationship, he

became more centrally involved with the Comintern's propaganda work and spent periods in Paris, Geneva and Prague as
diplomatic correspondent for the *Daily Worker*; Koltsov
then appointed him as *Pravda*'s first London correspondent. This
job only lasted a short while before Koltsov disappeared in one of
Stalin's purges after being recalled to Moscow from Barcelona.

In this sense, his work in Spain was only covering one act in a
longer play, one that was to end with the declaration of war in
1939. He saw this himself when he went to Prague to cover the
Sudeten crisis in 1938, pointing out that

> It seemed as though half of the international figures one had known in
> Madrid had assembled in Prague, and the sight of them seemed
> ominous. You felt there would soon have to be shells cracking against
> the hotel to complete the picture. It reminded one of the story of the
> famous Hearst reporter, specialist in political disasters, H.R.
> Knickerbocker, when he came to Vienna at some moment of crisis.
> 'Good God!' cried the hotel manager. '*You* here, Herr Knickerbocker?
> Is it then already so bad?' It looked like the end of an act, and it was.

Cockburn in Spain was everything that Knickerbocker was
not. Although the outcome of the war was a disaster for Spain
and for the rest of Europe, he told the story of the early days of
heroic optimism in a series of remarkable despatches. In
subsequent writing about the press coverage of the war, the
question has been raised about the accuracy of some reports,
most recently by the distinguished investigative journalist Philip
Knightly in his book on the history of war correspondents, *The
First Casualty*. He accuses Cockburn – along with many other
correspondents in modern wars, it should be said – of bias and
the occasional invention of material to suit the exigencies of the
moment. Whatever may have happened in any one particular
case, which in the nature of things is unlikely ever to be known
exactly, Knightly's charge is not new, but reflects a
long-standing controversy about the job of a war correspondent,
and perhaps of all journalists. The modern conception of a war
reporter, in Knightly's terms, is of an Olympian figure removed
from the fray, without prejudices or opinions of his own. To
many this has seemed an impossible ideal, an empty liberal
fiction. In the context of Spain it is best answered by Herbert
Matthews, the correspondent of the *New York Times*:

> All of us who lived in the Spanish Civil War felt deeply emotional
> about it ... I always felt the falseness and hypocrisy of those who
> claimed to be unbiased, and the foolish, if not rank stupidity of editors

and readers who demand objectivity or impartiality of correspondents writing about the war ... it was the same old error which readers and editors will always make and which forever continues to plague the chronicler who, being human, must have his feelings and opinions; in condemning bias one rejects the only factors which really matter – honesty, understanding and thoroughness.

In this sense, Cockburn was a great reporter, even if, like most other correspondents there, he was sometimes guilty of over-optimism. Some things didn't happen as they were predicted, others went badly when they were written up as dead heats or partial victories. Almost all writers, on both sides, confused hope with reality. But the great distinction in his work in Spain was to see combat through the eyes of the ordinary soldier in appallingly difficult circumstances, and never to lose sight of the reasons why he was there. In this respect he followed in the great tradition established by Russell in the Crimea, and the other nineteenth-century founders of the trade. He wrote himself, some years later:

> Naturally, the role of the intellectuals, the troubles and dissensions and heroisms of the intellectuals, were in reality matters of insignificance compared to the troubles, dissensions and heroisms of the men who mainly fought the war – and they ranged from peasants out of Almanza, who walked all the way to Madrid to fight, to a steel-worker from Budapest who travelled all night hanging on to the undercarriage of the Orient Express so as to get to Paris and be sent on to fight, to men from Glasgow and Liverpool and Brooklyn and San Francisco who gave up everything they had to go out there and fight.
>
> Nobody under the age of about thirty-five today has much notion of what the Spanish War meant to the people of that distant period in which it was fought, and nobody over that age will agree with any generalisation anyone makes about it. I personally disagree with about half the generalisations I made about it at the time. Rather than tussle with all that, it is better perhaps – for the moment at least – to remember some pictures.

The purpose of this book is to bring some of the pictures, that, in those days were seen in Britain by readers of the *Daily Worker* in the bus queue, the factory canteen or the home, back to life.

BIOGRAPHICAL NOTE

Claud Cockburn was born in Peking, in 1904, the son of a diplomatic family, and educated at Berkhamsted School and the

universities of Oxford, Budapest and Berlin. He became a
journalist on *The Times* while still in Berlin, subsequently
moving to the paper's New York office. He resigned in 1933 to
found *The Week*, which he edited until it was banned for some
eighteen months during the Second World War; its publication
ceased shortly after the war. He was a special correspondent for
the *Daily Worker* in the same period, and became its diplomatic
correspondent. He moved to Ireland in 1947, and contributed to
various newspapers and periodicals, as well as writing five
novels, several books of non-fiction and three volumes of
autobiography collected under the title, *I, Claud.* He was a
formative influence on the magazine *Private Eye*, and wrote a
weekly column for the *Irish Times* until his death in December
1981.

BOOKS BY CLAUD COCKBURN

High Low Washington 1930–32 1932
Reporter in Spain (Frank Pitcairn) 1936
Beat the Devil (James Helvick) 1953
Overdraft on Glory (James Helvick) 1955
Nine Bald Men 1956
In Time of Trouble 1956
Aspects of English History 1957
Crossing the Line 1958
The Horses (James Helvick) 1961
View From the West 1967
I, Claud (collected autobiography comprising *In Time of
Trouble, Crossing the Line* and *View From the West*) 1967
Ballantyne's Folly 1970
Bestseller 1972
The Devil's Decade 1973
Jericho Road 1974
Mr Mintoff Comes to Ireland 1975
Union Power 1976
The Peace-seeker's Tale 1981
Cockburn Sums Up 1981

Editorial Note

When he was writing for the *Daily Worker*, Claud Cockburn always wrote under the name of Frank Pitcairn, a pseudonym he also used when writing in other papers published in China, Eastern Europe and the USA. When he became the *Daily Worker*'s correspondent in Spain, material usually appeared under this by-line. He is, however, sometimes referred to as a 'Special Correspondent', and later on in 1937 and 1938, when he became the paper's diplomatic correspondent, as such. I have not used material when he is not named as Frank Pitcairn, except in one or two cases where it seems to be absolutely clear, by style and context, that he filed the copy in question. This usually took place when, because of poor communications with Spain, the paper had to run part of a story based on agency reports, but was able to supplement it with Pitcairn's later copy. The problems of communication, in general, should be borne in mind by the reader, as they affected all correspondents and as they affected readers' perceptions of events. For instance, the *Daily Worker* did not publish a reasonably complete list of the fallen at the Battle of Jarama in which so many British volunteers died, until July 1937, five months after the fighting.

The headlines are as printed in the *Daily Worker*, but in most cases I have retained only the main head as the *Daily Worker* followed the practice of the time in often using three or four headlines for its main stories. It is probable that the great majority of these headlines were written by Allen Hutt, then chief sub-editor on the paper. All sub-headlines used in the paper have been deleted.

A few Spanish spellings and obvious typographical errors at the *Daily Worker* and in *Reporter in Spain* have been corrected; otherwise, the material here is reprinted unaltered from the way it first appeared.

I would like to thank Stephen Hayward for his invaluable assistance.

Chapter One

RESISTANCE

In the early part of Reporter in Spain, *Cockburn describes the atmosphere in Spain before the officers' revolt had developed into a full-scale armed rebellion with foreign support, and draws on material he had been unable to use in the first hurried despatches he had telephoned back to London after his arrival in Spain in July 1936. In the despatches which follow the opening chapters of* Reporter in Spain, *Cockburn describes his involvement in the fighting that was developing around Madrid, and the efforts the Republican government was making to defend the city. As well as sending material to the* Daily Worker, *he was also continuing to contribute suitable material to* The Week, *two examples of which are included, his description of popular power in Barcelona and a brilliant pen portrait of a British diplomat in Madrid.*

I

By July you did not need to enter Spain to know that 'something was going to happen.' Ticker-tape carried news of murder by day and murder by night, as tommy-guns, automatics and bombs registered the violent answer of the Right to the February election victory of the democrats.

In the frontier villages and townships on the French side already there was 'something in the air'.

On 12 July I breakfasted in the station restaurant at Cerbère. I knew the waiter from the days when he had given me some useful tips about getting into Spain during the anti-fascist general strike of October 1934.

Across the restaurant came a pungent smell of violets. A tall fattish man with a waddling gait and expensive clothes walked in and around, and out, and in again to a table.

Two younger men walked beside him. 'Bodyguard' was written all over them. I have seen the same type walking with the big gangsters in Los Angeles back in the prohibition time. They inclined their heads like attachés in expectation of an order.

One, with the customary dress-habits of the gangster, wore an absurdly tight-cut Palm Beach suit which showed the gun on his hip.

The fat man gently rolled that violet scented handkerchief in his stout hands and kept his eye on the door.

The noise of a train rolling through the tunnel under the mountain from the Spanish side brought the fat man to his feet. The trio left.

'Somebody in particular?' I asked the waiter.

'They say so,' said he.

'Well and?'

'A Colonel something or other from Madrid. Big shot. Has an aeroplane up in Perpignan. Colonel of aviation I think. Lives at the Grand Hotel. Very swell.'

'So what?'

'So nothing. Except that they say – I'm just telling you what they say – that he isn't there for nothing, so to speak. Possibly you understand something of the situation in Spain.'

'Well?'

'Well a fortnight ago this fellow comes hell for leather over the frontier at Le Perthus, by car of course, and goes up to Perpignan at the Grand Hotel. He was mixed up some way in killing the miners in Asturias last year and the year before or whenever it was. That's why he had to beat it after the elections. They say he has a mission.'

'Such as?'

'How should I know? I suppose you and I think the rich are going to sit quiet and – what's the phrase? – "accept the verdict of the pee-pull?" Like hell they are.'

'This is the twelfth of July. Five months after the elections.'

'All the longer to get ready.'

'So the Colonel, what is he doing down here on the frontier?'

'Well, I should say, and our Spanish comrades here say that he is, so to speak, listening for something.'

'Listening?'

He made a gesture, indicating a man putting his ear to the ground.

'You think he'll hear something soon?'

He grimaced, and I had to be going.

When the train moved into Spain, the Fascist Colonel was

standing on the opposite platform. Expensive and perfumed, with his sleek gunmen bodyguard, listening for news of a steadily thickening plot against his country, he reminded me suddenly of Hungarian right-wing officers I had seen in Vienna during the Communist regime in Budapest.

They used to sit in the Hotel Sacher, plotting with the Romanians about the Romanian invasion of their country.

It occurred to me that if you wanted a 1936 symbol of 'Death', like the stock figure of death in medieval paintings, the Colonel would do.

II

That was around nine o'clock on the morning of 12 July. Twelve hours later gunmen in a touring car nosed slowly through sparse traffic under the arc lamps of a Madrid street, opened fire with a sub-machine-gun at the defenceless back of a man standing chatting on his doorstep, and roared off among the tram-lines, leaving him dying in a puddle of his young blood on the pavement.

That in a manner of speaking was the Sarajevo of the Spanish war. The young man they killed was José Castillo, Lieutenant of Assault Guards. I never saw Castillo, but afterwards I heard all sorts of people speak of him with a kind of urgency and heartbreak, as though it were impossible that you too should not have known, and therefore loved, so fine a young man.

In a corps which in the five years of its existence had already acquired a high military reputation, Castillo was already distinguished, and already loved, by men who are not very easy pleased nor easy fooled.

In the working-class districts of Madrid he was equally well known and liked. He was declared a gallant and patriotic young officer, as dauntless a defender of the Republic as you could wish to see, and a man – as a Madrid workman said to me afterwards – 'who made the culture and the progress we were after seem more real to us'.

In April there had been rioting, organised against the newly formed government elected by the people at the February elections.

It was an affair of gunmen, snipers, professional bomb-throwers, hired to do a job of simply creating disorder in the capital.

For the Right, following the elections, order was fatal; disorder at worst a small tactical success, at best an opportunity. Among those who at that time felt the weight of Lieutenant Castillo's efforts on behalf of law and order against gunman outrage in Madrid was a close relative of no less a personage than Calvo Sotelo.

An aristocrat, rich man, and able political boss, Sotelo was far more able, and probably more powerful in their counsels, than Gil Robles himself.

When in mid-June Castillo was about to marry, his fiancée, a girl even younger than himself, got a note from Calvo Sotelo's headquarters. It said:

'Do not marry Castillo. He is for it. He is on our list. You will be a widow within a month. You have been warned.'

She married Castillo, and while a hot June blazed into a hotter July, the crime sheets in the Madrid police department multiplied daily, as the gunmen of the parties defeated at the ballot went about their horrid business, sometimes by night, sometimes in broad daylight.

Once, they shot tommy-guns into a crowd of unarmed citizens leaving a meeting. Often they threw bombs. Instructions were found directing certain criminal elements to acquire immediate membership in the CNT (anarcho-syndicalist union) in order to have an opportunity to provoke acts of violence.

Sometimes they succeeded. In the way of provocation, people can stand just so much, depending on the degree of their political understanding, political discipline, and actual organisational control of undesirable hostile elements worming their way into their organisations. If everyone were proof against provocation there would be no provocateurs and the enemy would find another weapon.

Some time before midnight on the night Castillo was shot, the Assault Guards of his troop in Madrid had already decided to carry out, immediately and without waiting for action from above, the arrest of Calvo Sotelo.

Determined that this time the 'man behind the man behind the gun' was going to answer for the crime, they were in a state of extreme anxiety lest Calvo Sotelo himself – with vast financial resources behind him – might either buy immunity in Madrid, or escape the country, leaving some underling to hold the bag.

In the early hours of the morning a police car, under command of a Lieutenant Moreno, drove out to Sotelo's house, got him out of bed and told him he was under arrest.

Cornered, but still hopeful that the Sotelo money could 'fix' one crime more, Sotelo tried to telephone to friends, and government officials. The Assault Guards, the friends of Castillo, were impatient.

They foresaw already a long series of legal delays, ending with a probable escape of the murderer. They stuck to the original plan of taking him under arrest to the station house, and there presenting the authorities with a *fait accompli*, figuring it would be very much more difficult for anyone to order the release of Sotelo once he was arrested than it would be to prevent him being arrested at all.

They put him in the police car.

The car shot off in the direction of the station house. Of what happened next I have heard several conflicting versions, one from a man who was actually in the car at the time. He stated that another car, moving fast without lights, was heard racing behind them, that they prepared for action against an attempt at armed release of the prisoner, and that at the last moment a young Assault Guard, losing his head and thinking that Sotelo might escape them yet, put a bullet through the back of that subtle politician's head.

In any case, the car drew up half-way to the barracks, and somebody, looking over Sotelo's body said, 'The only place we can go now is the cemetery.'

They drove to the cemetery, deposited the body with the night watchman, and drove off. When they reached the station house Lieutenant Moreno was in a state of collapse.

Declaring that he and he alone had been responsible for the safety of the prisoner under his charge, and that nothing but his own death could expiate the disgrace of what had happened, he made an immediate attempt at suicide, as soon as he had completed his report.

They knocked the gun out of his hand.

For hours in the dawning light, they argued with him, telling him that whatever had happened, another death could neither improve nor alter the grim situation of the facts as they now were.

They urged that Moreno must immediately leave the country,

since in Spain he would be under sentence of death from the
Sotelo organisation. Moreno, watching that fateful dawn break
over Madrid, declared he would stay and face death that way;
suicide attempt number two.

An American offered him a passport. He refused. In a state of
extreme agony of mind Moreno agreed to be taken into hiding in
Madrid, but refused to leave the country.

Nine days later he was in the very first car which dashed over
the sierras to meet the rebel attack on Madrid. He was found
dead in the mountains, far in advance of the line of the
government forces, riddled with bullets, his face to the enemy.

Thus Lieutenant Moreno settled his score with himself.

III

Barcelona was gay that weekend with the big brilliantly coloured
posters of the People's Olympiad. We were pretty tired and sat
down to drink coffee on the terrace of the Hotel Colón, and
watch the crowd go by on the Plaza Catalunya.

I remembered the last time I sat there, in October 1934. There
were machine guns outside the entrance to the Telephone
Exchange across the way, and a mob of international journalists
hung about anxious and tired on the terrace waiting for
telephone calls to get through to London. Reuter's man got
through and came out, talking excitedly. There was a flutter and
a kind of a gasp as the story he had just heard from London
flashed along the terrace.

It was the news of the killing of Bertou and Alexander of
Jugoslavia at Marseilles.* We did not know then the grim
background of that murder; the figures of the background –
Rosenberg, the Gestapo, the Italian secret police were still well
concealed in the shadows. We knew nothing even of the secret
meeting in Munich where the fatal guns were handed over. We
only saw the shadow of the gunman lengthen suddenly across

---

* King Alexander of Yugoslavia was assassinated in October 1934 when visiting
France, together with Dr Bertou, a French official. A group of militant Croat
nationalists was responsible, members of the *ustaš a* led by Ante Pavelić who were
subsequently given refuge in Fascist Italy and encouraged to plot the downfall of the
independent Yugoslav state.

Europe, and for a moment of keen vision everyone saw quite sharply and clearly what Europe was up against.

In the moment of cold shock even the dullest saw and remarked that political terrorism had to be regarded as a recognised instrument in the routine policy of 'certain powers'.

Today, the news of the murder of Castillo and close upon it the news of how Castillo's comrades in arms had settled accounts with Calvo Sotelo came suddenly over the wires from Madrid and in half an hour, despite a heavily censored press, was circulating through the city like the ugly warning of an air-raid siren.

On the Rambla I heard myself hailed from an upper window. A comrade, artist, union organiser and fighting man, came bounding down the stairs of the engravers' union offices.

I had scarcely seen him since we stood together one day in the fruit market at Burnley and he drew uncomplimentary pictures of a loud-mouthed Fascist ex-officer haranguing half-starved weavers from an empty champagne case. He was an exile then, just escaped from Gil Robles' prison ship in Barcelona harbour where he had been imprisoned for his share in the anti-fascist strike of 1934.

'Bit of a change?'

He shrugged and fluttered his hand in the Spanish gesture which means that anything may happen. He showed me a scrawled note someone had poked through the door. It said:

'Get out of Barcelona. You have twenty-four hours' notice to quit. The alternative is death.' He explained that Fascist gunmen were going round all the union offices threatening the militant officials with death. 'Taking one thing with another,' he said, 'I think the barometer is at storm.'

Without looking up from the paper he was reading another man in the office said gently, 'And yet to think there are people running round loose in this town who imagine because we won the elections the enemy is done for. We shall see.'

'And in England?' said this comrade. 'How are things?'

I began to tell him. He was always a rather impatient man and when I told them that the role of certain Labour leaders in splitting the labour movement in the face of the Fascist danger was still unchanged, and even intensified, he jumped out of his chair and walked about the room, snapping his fingers.

The other man said, 'But don't they understand anything? Don't they learn anything from our example and the French?'

I told them some stories about the *Daily Herald*; they said, 'If it didn't make you cry it would make you laugh.' They asked how Caballero's plea for unity at the International Federation of Trades Unions had been received. We discussed that a little and I asked some more about the latest news from Madrid. 'The attack', they said, 'is coming. If you want some holiday and some rest you had better get it quickly. Go down the coast and bathe and be ready for anything.'

'You understand', said the other man, 'that there are a lot of people living in a pipe dream. It's natural enough. They worked hard for unity and the People's Front and they think that now we've won the elections the others will sit back and let us get on with setting up a real democracy in this country. But you don't get democracy on the cheap.'

IV

We took that advice and went down the coast to Salou to rest and bathe. It was a tiny village where the plain met the sea, with two streets, houses half-buried in bougainvillaea and sweet honeysuckle, a few ornate little villas, a terraced beach café with a red dome made out of corrugated iron, and seven miles of perfect white sand, entirely deserted.

In the bungalow hotel-restaurant by the station there were tables laid for forty, but when it came to meal-time we were the only guests. The waiter, who was the same waiter who worked afternoons at the beach café, put on a white coat and brought dinner to us among the empty tables as though he were unconscious of them and their emptiness. You felt as though you were taking part in some elaborate play, in a scene set for something just going to happen.

The waiter, a member of the UGT, whose home was in Reus, a few miles inland, was at first notably cautious. Even there among the honeysuckle on that deserted terrace you had the impression that now was a time when any man not known to be a friend might be an enemy.

Even there you could see the barometer moving to storm.

It was in those days that General Sanjurjo was hurrying back from Berlin after urgent talks with Hitler, and General Franco's

emissaries were already on their way back to Morocco from
Rome.

'Is the place ordinarily so empty at this time of year?' we
asked non-committally.

'No,' he said, 'it isn't. Ordinarily quite a lot of rich people
come down from Madrid to the villas down here and spend a bit
of money.'

'So why aren't they here now?'

He made the same gesture with his hand that I had seen
made, indicating a situation in which anything may happen.

'Some of them have gone to France this year I understand,' he
said cautiously.

'You mean they can't seem to settle down to democracy,' I
suggested.

He looked at me with more confidence and smiled. 'That's
just about it,' he said. 'It's not right the way such people go on.
They had their chance. Now we get together and make
democracy here in Spain, we win the elections, and they want to
wreck everything.'

We had a drink together and he talked. He was a very young
man, and the political news that filtered through to that desolate
village was sparse and confusing. He had to repeat over and
over the main facts of the situation as he saw it, asking us
whether it was not so, and if so, why was it so. He knew well
enough from first hand experience what the Church and the rich
reactionaries were like, and yet it seemed to him, that after the
election victory somehow they ought to have accepted things
and let decent folk get on with their business in peace.

I thought of what the man in Barcelona had said about people
living in a pipe dream.

'In some of the villages around here,' he said, leaning forward
and whispering, 'the priests are going round giving money out of
a bag to all sorts of riff-raff, corner-boys and loafers and thieves.
They tell them that if only the People's Front were done for, they
would get easy money like that all the time.'

Oddly enough, that was first hand confirmation of something
Alvarez del Vayo had told me at the Premier Hotel in Russell
Square, only a few days before. The Church, he had said, the
largest landowner in Spain, had begun converting real estate into
cash on a huge scale, and was using the cash in an extraordinary
bribery campaign, sending priests round with largesse for
corner-boys and criminals exactly as the waiter now described.

Vayo had pointed to that as one of the clearest indications of the attack that was coming on the united forces of the young Spanish democracy. I told him that a week before, leading acceptance houses in the City of London had received a sudden notification from the Bank of England telling them to close up on all Spanish commitments. It was like hearing the stealthy movement of huge forces moving up to a night attack.

That same afternoon, the staff of the Communist *Mundo Obrero* newspaper in Madrid applied to the government for a permit for twelve pistols to defend the office against violent assault by Fascists. The permit was granted and they took it in turns to stand guard at the office all night.

In Barcelona, the Communists, sure that the attack was coming almost at once, urged certain precautions upon the government, which declined, declaring that the danger was exaggerated. Failing government action, small groups of trade unionists and members of the United Socialist and youth organisations patrolled the Ramblas that night, ready to give an alarm.

The next afternoon we saw that the number of the Civil Guards at Salou had been doubled. They stood about, conspicuous and with nothing to do yet, adding to the atmosphere of oppressive expectancy which must have been felt that week in every village of Spain, as the democracy, newly won by the unity of all the forces of progress, slowly gathered itself into an attitude of defence against the blow being visibly prepared.

V

On the Saturday morning (18 July), the trade union committees of the Workers' Alliance, particularly the railwaymen, in Madrid and Barcelona, sent an urgent call to all members to pass by the committee rooms that day.

They came and were given a warning not to leave town on the Sunday, cancelling all holiday arrangements for the day. It was decided by the railwaymen to put the warning into practical effect by cancelling all cheap workers' trains out of the big cities that Sunday.

There was at this point a characteristic difference in the estimate of the situation as made by the working-class organisations and the government. The government, with a mass of data at its disposal, still certainly underestimated, as it did at intervals throughout the first weeks of the war, the full extent and character of the movement that had been launched against it.

It supposed up to the last minute that ordinary police measures would be sufficient to deal with anything that might happen, displaying a certain '*pipe-dream*' confidence in the solidity of a regime elected and supported by the democratic votes of the people, in the face of an organised attack by the forces of the reaction.

The working-class organisations on the other hand, with less immediate data to go upon, but of very much superior political education and theoretical grasp of political realities, knew with absolute certainty, first, that the attack would come, and secondly, that it would be of a character no less violent, ruthless and formidable than – for instance – Dollfuss's attack on the working people of Vienna in 1934.

During that Saturday, government radio stations broadcast repeatedly the official communiqué on the rising in Morocco. At the time I did not understand why the radio communiqué insisted so emphatically on the statement that despite rumours to the contrary, no 'state of war' had been proclaimed in any part of Spain.

I supposed that this was simply a bit of propagandist reassurance to the public. It, in fact, had a more practical aim. The rebels, by direct word of mouth and from certain radio stations of which they had already seized temporary control, had announced a 'state of war' with the idea of paralysing in advance any working-class action in defence of the Republic – particularly the general strike. For a state of war automatically cancels the freedom of action of working-class organisations and enables the military command to assume more or less direct control of the workers, particularly in the essential services such as railways, transport, light and power.

In the early hours of Sunday morning I boarded at Salou what I thought was just the early north express and turned out to be the last peace-time train that reached Barcelona.

At Sitges, a group of boys stood on the deserted golf course, constructed to attract the British tourists at the moment

cramming the hotels of that famous beauty spot of the Spanish
Riviera, and shouted at us that there was shooting in Barcelona.

At the stopping places beyond Sitges, all along the line of
coastal villages, people began to surge round the train, shouting
out the news as it had come through the railway telephone
service.

At first people in the train stood silent, or murmuring to one
another as the news of the attack sank in and became real. A
few hours before they had been simply a trainload of casual
people in their Sunday best going up to pay a visit to friends and
relations in Barcelona. Now suddenly they were people under
attack.

There was a murmur and a hum of excited anxious voices.
Then a young bank clerk, standing in his newly pressed Sunday
suit in the crowded third-class corridor beside me leaned from
the window and shouted to all the world:

'Long Live the Republic!'

As the shout rang out over the little station, railwaymen,
peasant women, fisherfolk, clerks and businessmen and hotel
porters surged forward towards the train, the people in the train
leaned out to meet them, and in unity they all took up the cry
together. People shook hands with people they had never seen
before and called them 'Comrade', and as the train pulled on
towards Barcelona, 'Long Live Democracy! Long Live the
Republic!' thundered all up and down its corridors.

The train crawled forward, stopped and crawled on again.
Sometimes the word was passed down to lie flat on the floor as
there would be shooting on the line. Then would come an 'all
clear' and everyone hung out of the windows trying to peer
forward towards Barcelona.

The reason for the delay and the uncertainty was the fact that
at that very moment the people of Sants, the south-westerly
working-class suburb of Barcelona, were fighting for the streets
and the station with the troops who at dawn had suddenly
advanced on them from the barracks up the hill.

In that bloody and heroic dawn, all over Spain people pulled
suddenly from their beds were fighting with pistols and
shot-guns and bare hands against fully-equipped soldiers led
against them by officers who for weeks had listened for the
signal for treachery to come into the open.

We pulled into Sants amid a thunder of cheers rolling up and
down the station and down from the streets overlooking the

embankment told of victory. The train went no further, and I walked across Barcelona in the beautiful freshness and light of the early southern morning, with the noise of rifle and machine-gun fire growing louder and louder as I came towards the centre of the city. Crowds of people, some of them still only half-dressed, and some with their heads bandaged and pistols in their hands stood listening in tense silence to the radio news bulletins from the loudspeakers in the pavement cafés and bars.

I came round the corner by the School of Medicine and saw the first ambulances dashing up from the Plaza Catalunya, and inside the place a horde of medical students working with desperate speed to dress the wounds of those first casualties in the front line defences of our democracy.

VI

Looking back, it would appear obvious that the situation of the men and women who rushed out that morning to defend themselves and their towns against the army attack was quite hopeless.

It did not occur however to the sleepy and mostly unarmed men who rushed the Montaña barracks in Madrid against all the rifles and machine guns of the biggest garrison in Spain, that by all the laws of war they could never take those barracks.

They took them, and when they got inside they saw a line of twenty or thirty officers with big automatic pistols, lined up behind a parapet, green and shaking not with fear only, but with astonishment, at the huge heroism of the people who had thrown themselves against the machine-gun emplacements and the riflemen, and broken their way in against odds which were intended to be, and ought to have been, overwhelming.

The half-dozen men who held the inside of the telephone building at Barcelona, the three who held the radio station against a whole troop of Fascist officers, that white-haired Communist woman, Caridad Mercadet, who led a little band of men and women with rifles, sporting guns and two airguns against the Army Command building at the bottom of the Rambla, did not, it seems, grasp that such things are impossible.

The officers who planned the betrayal of Spain thought, and

admitted afterwards that they had thought, the thing impossible. They thought they would have a walk-over. They had, and they admitted it, no remote notion of the heights of courage and tenacity of which the people, once united in defence of democracy and the most elementary rights of humanity, is capable. It was only days later, when defeat at the hands of the people stared them in the face, that they realised treachery must go further and deeper, and opening the gates of their country wider still to the enemy, called for new reinforcements from Germany, Italy and the Moors, just as French grandees had tried to betray France to foreign enemies against the French people more than a hundred years before.

I came out that Sunday morning into Hospital Street and saw tense-faced boys and girls, clutching miserable old weapons, including a number of broken airguns taken from a sporting gun shop, advancing slowly but unwaveringly up the pavements against a towering red-brick church with sandbagged loopholes in its walls from which a machine-gun and a score or more of modern army rifles cracked and spat continuously.

A boy fell over suddenly on the pavement and rolled into the roadway. A girl bent hurriedly over him. He whispered something. She took the Republican emblem from her arm and gave it to him and he kissed it and so died. The advance went on.

It did not occur to me then that the boy who died under a priest's rifle fire in Hospital Street was shortly to be accused in the British reactionary press of 'an outrageous attack on a Church' and reminded that to use violence against priests is a barbarous act, forfeiting the respect and support of respectable people.

We thought that when the Church takes up arms against the people, the people has the right to defend itself even against priests.

You only had to twiddle the radio knobs to hear something of what was happening in the places where the people had failed in their defence. You tuned into Seville, and heard drunken General Queipo de Llano hiccuping out his endless ugly polemic against civilisation, progress and democracy. In Seville, the democrats got no arms, and in the poorest quarter of the city they held out for four days fighting street-to-street, house-to-house, room-to-room, with knives and boiling oil.

The women heated the oil, and under the volleys of rifle fire brought it in jugs and saucepans and slop-pails to the men lodged on window ledges and the angles of roofs, whence they poured it down on advancing soldiery.

They died fighting, and the others – who had not died in that first struggle for the city – were massacred and many of them burned alive later, when the Generals met at Cadiz to plan a northern drive with the Moors and agreed that the wiping out of the working population of Andalusia was a military necessity 'to keep the country quiet'.

Turn the knobs again and hear what the Generals have to say to you. Here is Franco, there is Mola, and there Cabanellas, all roaring into the microphones in a nightmare chorus of things to come, filling the air of tortured Europe with the menace of the warlords, the horror of great darkness, spitting fire and slaughter and slavery, the Brasshats and the Inquisitors and the enemies of the people, marching on.

VII

Driven from their main positions by the frontal attack of the armed people, Fascist gunmen took to the roofs, particularly the roofs of the churches, and sniped at people in the street.

They had considerable success. They fired indiscriminately, as I was able to observe from a good deal of personal experience, at armed men and at women going to market. Men in the street with rifles often got the jumps as the firing went on, and started to fire back indiscriminately at the windows and roofs where they thought the shots were coming from. Several churches were fired as the gunmen made good their escape over the roofs.

I went to the central post office to send a press telegram and took half an hour doing it, being stopped continuously by rifle fire from the roofs. Later we saw militiamen and Assault Guards running along the roofs, cleaning them up.

Painfully, but quickly, order began to be brought back to the great city. Patrol cars rushed through the streets, foot patrols guarded the corners and watched the roofs for gunmen, the first orders against looting and the first shooting of criminals who did loot occurred within a few hours of one another. On public buildings appeared the notice which soon was to appear in one form or another on buildings of artistic or historical interest throughout the government-controlled areas of the country:

'Citizens, this building is now your property. Take care of it. Respect it. See that others do so too.'

Felicia Browne, the English artist, who afterwards died, shot through the head as she worked a machine-gun at Tardienta, went that day to see the British Consulate about some papers that had to be signed in connection with a motor-car smash outside Barcelona just before the rebellion began.

'A period of unbridled licence', the consular official told her gravely, 'has begun.'

He also stated with considerable glee that a rebel column was already marching on Barcelona from Saragossa – a fact which was untrue but was being spread assiduously through the city by Fascist agents with the same purpose which directed the fire of the gunmen on the roofs; the creation of panic and disorder.

It was at all times curious how closely the stories retailed by British diplomatic and consular officials in Spain tallied with the stories being manufactured by the agents of the enemy.

Daily Worker, 23 July 1936

EYE WITNESS STORY OF BARCELONA

How Workers' Power Smashed Fascism

Thursday, 23 July, 1936.

This story was telephoned last night by our special correspondent, Frank Pitcairn, who was an eye-witness of the events in Barcelona, and who made a motor-car dash to the French frontier to get telephonic communication with the Daily Worker.

He has returned to Barcelona, and will later send further reports of the Spanish people's great fight to crush the Fascist revolt.

Spain is living through the most momentous hours of its long revolutionary history.

The situation is unprecedented. Against the bloody Fascist attack and in defence of democracy a whole people has sprung to arms.

At the very first alarm men and women, transport workers, miners, printers, builders, engineers, clerks, typists, and shopkeepers literally rushed into the streets.

Most of them were unarmed. Some were armed with nothing better than shot-guns, antique revolvers, and even air-guns.

Today they have at least a fair number of rifles, modern pistols, machine-guns and field guns, taken in combat from the enemy.

Decisive events of the last day and night are:-

1) Acceptance by all Left parties of the Communist Party's proposal for immediate organisation of an armed workers' militia of the people against Fascism. Thus from this vast spontaneous mass which came into being almost overnight is at this moment being formed a properly organised army and trained force of disciplined fighters.

2) The formation in Barcelona of a committee for the defence of Barcelona against Fascism wherein all Left parties and trade unions, including the anarchists, are being represented. The general position is as follows:

The workers have smashed the attack in almost all the main centres of the country, including Madrid, Barcelona, Malaga, Asturias and Valencia.

Fighting reached its peak in Barcelona, where there were reckoned to be 200 dead and something like a thousand wounded in the defence of the people and the Spanish Republic against the onslaught of the Fascist officers.

Fighting is still going on in Seville and Saragossa. From Saragossa a Fascist column is reported to be marching towards Barcelona.

A large force of workers has set out from Barcelona to meet them. At the same time the leaders of the working-class organisations in Catalonia are broadcasting encouragement to those under the Fascist terror in Saragossa.

On the side of the workers have fought the Civil Guards and Assault Guards, and in most cases the rank and file of the police.

Scores of thousands of common soldiers refused to follow the orders of the Fascist officers. Some shot their officers almost immediately, some went over to the workers, some simply went home.

Late last night I left Barcelona in one of the cars requisitioned for transport by the Communist Party.

The other occupants were carrying directions from the Centre in Barcelona to the local committees between there and the frontier.

With rifles permanently at the ready and safety catches off, we drove across a whole countryside in arms. For miles outside Barcelona there were barricades every half-mile.

Thousands of armed workers are guarding every road. A control of permits is carried out strictly and efficiently.

Local committees along the road distributed cards directing the hotels and cafés to supply food and lodging. Alike, in fair-size towns and little lost villages along, the volunteers are out.

While permits were examined we exchanged news of Barcelona and the local events.

At a tiny village, a middle-aged farm worker showed us his aged shot-gun, and inquired what the chances were for getting better weapons for himself and the local comrades.

At Gerona last night, the capital of that section of the province, I watched the distribution of arms in the Town Hall.

It was a magnificent sight to see the workers drawn up to receive their rifles beneath the ancient panelled roof and golden candelabra of the centre of government of the district.

The military attack in Barcelona began in the early hours of Sunday morning.

Three regiments were involved – including a cavalry regiment.

At 5.15 troops from the barracks behind the city appeared on Catalonia Square, which lies at the centre of Barcelona on the top of the wide avenue leading down to the docks.

On the west and south side of the square are big hotels. On the north-east corner stands the central telephone building, which was the first Fascist objective.

The officers were already in occupation of the arsenal and the army headquarters which lie by the docks opposite to the main avenue half a mile or more from Catalonia Square.

Owing to the fact that the government had refused to take seriously Communist warnings of the coming Fascist attack, the workers on the square and at the top of the avenue were few and badly-armed.

With them were a sprinkling of well-armed Assault Guards and police. There was a moment of suspense as the officers faced one another across the square.

Suddenly the soldiers broke their ranks, and shouting, 'Long live the Republic' ran across the square waving their weapons in the air, to fraternise with the workers.

The workers greeted them joyously, and for some moments there was a happy scene as soldiers and workers moved across the square, shouting and cheering with their arms round one another's shoulders.

Casually, the whole group began to drift across the square in the direction of the telephone building. They were within a few yards of the door, when a sudden change came across the situation.

A man who had been standing with his arm around the neck of one of the Assault Guards suddenly whipped out his pistol and fired point-blank, killing the guard on the spot.

A worker brought his rifle smashing down on the head of the assailant. The shot had been fired. It was the prearranged signal.

'Soldiers' who had 'fraternised' so pleasantly with the workers were far from being Communist soldiers and NCOs. They were, in fact, a picked corps of Fascist officers, who had adopted this trick to gain possession of the telephone building.

A moment after the firing of the murderous signal shot, the signal for the outbreak of Fascist violence which has caused hundreds of dead and wounded, furious fighting began at the door of the telephone building and a few minutes later at the broadcasting station round the corner.

Three men alone defended the station against the Fascists.

As a result of the 'fraternisation' trick, the Fascist officers got inside the door of the telephone building and hurled three hand-grenades into the midst of the group of workers inside the hall.

The workers were blown to pieces, but seven men in a heroic fight which lasted the greater part of the morning defended the telephone exchange so that although it was utterly wrecked by bombs and hand-grenades it never fell into the hands of the Fascists.

The moment the first news of the attack was heard in the city, the workers dashed into the streets. Badly-armed as they were, they had the terrific force of unity and common purpose to defend the city against Fascism.

Within a couple of hours of the first attack the streets were defended by a network of barricades manned by Communists, anarchists, Socialists and Republicans alike.

For the thirty-six hours the whole democratic population of Barcelona, led by a united working-class, fought the Fascists street by street and square by square.

The climax came with the storming of the arsenal on Monday afternoon. I myself saw workers armed at that time only with old-fashioned revolvers advancing down the street in the face of Fascist machine-guns trained on them from the arsenal where the Fascists had unlimited ammunition, and they were safe from bombardment from the air because it was feared that if the whole arsenal blew up the port might be permanently damaged.

Order has been re-established. When I left there last night hundreds of cars full of armed workers, storm guards and Civil Guards, were patrolling the streets. At all strategically important street corners there are barricades.

Lorries full of cheering workers are parading in the vicinity.

Stray Fascists and other criminals create an occasional diversion by shooting from the roofs. They appear to be being mopped up on the whole.

Daily Worker, 29 July 1936

HEAVY BLOWS AT REBELS

Saragossa Encircled

BARCELONA, Tuesday.

Five columns of democratic forces are now converging on Saragossa and are within twenty miles of the city.

Saragossa being probably the strongest strategic point in Spain, the struggle is likely to be fierce and possibly prolonged.

The city can only be approached across the river, and the bridges will certainly be blown up as the Fascists at present operating on the outskirts are forced to retreat into the city itself.

Fighting continues in the north-west at various points south of San Sebastian and in the neighbourhood of Oviedo.

On my way to the Saragossa front this weekend, in company with a delegate of the military commission, I toured villages and towns over a wide area between Barcelona and Lérida.

Everywhere I found calm confidence and swift progress as the workers develop their control of affairs in the defence against Fascism.

For example, at Targea the president of the local committee told me, 'The socialisation of all essential products has been an accomplished fact here since last Wednesday.

'Corn, olives, wine and all the other main agricultural produce of the area are now the property of the workers through their co-operative.

'This year's crops will be entirely owned by the poor peasants.

'It was first necessary to carry out the reorganisation of the landowners' co-operative which, until last week, consisted of both poor and rich peasants, with the latter naturally dominating policy.

'Now the big landowners, whose policy has been an obstacle to the placing of the food resources at the disposal of the people, have been rejected, with the result that the co-operative, which is entirely in the hands of the poor peasants, has taken over all the crops.'

These co-operatives work under the supreme control of the defence committee, on which the Workers' Alliance and the small bourgeois parties are also represented.

Throughout this area the workers have all returned to work. As a member of the committee in the small town of Agramunt explained, 'For the defence against Fascism it is essential that the fullest food supplies shall be available for the workers of Catalonia.

'If we don't work and produce, Barcelona will not eat.

'We are now working not for the rich, but for ourselves and for the workers of Barcelona and other cities of Catalonia.'

Barcelona also is mainly at work today. Trams and buses are running and shops providing necessaries are open.

There is strict control of prices and heavy fines are imposed for profiteering.

The anarchists have issued instructions for the formation of flying squads to deal with looters.

A bulletin issued by the anarchists points out the counter-revolutionary character of looting, particularly in its effect on shopkeepers who have been and are supporting the democratic forces.

The Week, No. 172, 29 July 1936

MEDITERRANEAN MADNESS?

Something in the nature of a major scare has been caused in well-informed quarters in London by the persistent circulation of a rumour, which, if true, might plunge Europe into immediate world war.

The report, briefly, is this:

General Franco, leader of the Spanish rebels, finding himself now in a somewhat unhappy position and faced with the prospect of defeat, has made a last-minute bid for Italian help against the existing Popular Front government of Spain.

The price offered is the cession to Italy of Ceuta (the port in Spanish Morocco) and the Balearic Island of Minorca.

From Spain

Our Barcelona correspondent telegraphs:

The Catalonian capital itself recalls General Nivelle's Parisian taxi-cab mobilisation in 1914. Thousands of workers and peasants, men and girls, are flocking into the city and presenting themselves at the barracks to be armed and equipped for the siege of Saragossa and neighbouring towns. Lorries, taxi-cabs and private cars are commandeered to carry those shock battalions into action. The railway workers volunteered to run trains into the interior with troops and supplies.

The exuberance is amazing. The city itself is quiet and orderly. In fact calm has been restored throughout Catalonia. Newspapers reappeared several days ago, casualty lists have been published, public services function smoothly under workers' control, cafés and places of entertainment have reopened. Accumulated foreign mails and newspapers have been distributed.

The probability is that a new government will be formed shortly in Madrid as well as Catalonia in which not only Socialists and trade unionists but also Communists and anarchists will be represented. In any case, it seems certain that the uprising has doomed the old army, which should have been disbanded long ago. An armed workers' militia, it is confidently predicted, will be a permanent feature of the country's defence and police force. The militia will co-operate closely with the Civil and Assault Guards.

Another certainty as soon as the rebels are crushed is that all working-class parties will demand drastic legislation along the following lines:

1. Confiscation of the property of all those directly or indirectly supporting the revolt. This includes the Jesuits and the Church.

2. The nationalisation of the large landed estates, the land to be divided among peasants, who shall get state aid to establish themselves.

3. State ownership and control of Spanish-owned industries. The creation of workers' councils in the factories.

Military committees composed of workers, soldiers and peasants and political leaders of the Left are already functioning in most cities and towns of Catalonia, in the Basque country and in various other parts.

Daily Worker, 30 July 1936

FASCISTS BOMB SPANISH WORKERS FROM FOREIGN PLANE

Stirring Scenes with Workers on March

Marching with the Republican forces on the road to Saragossa, our Special Correspondent was involved in a Fascist air raid from which he only narrowly escaped. Here is his thrilling story.

FRENCH FRONTIER, Wednesday.
I have just returned from the battle front of the high plain of Aragon, above Saragossa. Here, as one of our leaders said to me, is being fought out a pitched battle between the living future of Spain and the dead past, between the forces of freedom and the forces of Fascism and slavery.

I was present there during the first bomb attack upon the workers' columns by Fascist aeroplanes. Thirty-five bombs were dropped in that attack. I counted six dead and twenty-three more or less seriously wounded. One of the dead was a young woman worker from Barcelona.

I left shortly after the arrival of two aeroplanes from Barcelona had driven the Fascist planes away, and recovered command of the air for the democratic forces.

We joined the central column of the Barcelona workers legion after a breakneck drive from the mountain highway in which our first car was wrecked and the second turned out to have a broken gear-box. The third, a little four-seater Opel, was more successful.

We got our first views of the fighting when we reached the little town of Agramunt, near Lérida. Of the 4,000 inhabitants of Agramunt 500 are in the militia, and of these fifty have joined the columns marching to the relief of Saragossa.

I talked there to a mother of nine sons, five of whom are in the militia.

'They may die,' she said, 'we may die, but Fascism will not come to Catalonia.'

While we were talking in the offices of the Military Committee a telegram arrived from the Commander of the group which had gone from Agramunt to fight for freedom against Fascism. It said simply: 'We have taken Caspe.'

Caspe is a village on the high plateau above Saragossa. Black-shirted Fascists, in raiding parties from Saragossa, had for days been terrorising this whole plateau.

At Caspe they arrived and actually kidnapped twelve young men of the village, who were packed into cars on the point of the gun and driven off to Saragossa, being told they would have to fight there.

Later I talked to eye-witnesses of this scene. They told how Fascists arrived, terrorising a number of these villages. The local peasants fled into the fields, leaving their crops untended and their houses deserted.

As at Caspe, Fascists succeeded in capturing a number of women, whom they drove into the streets to act as a cover for their own flight when the workers' columns advanced upon them.

Owing to the fact that a number of anarchist battalions advanced too impetuously to clean up these villages, they suffered a number of unnecessary casualties. Then the organised forces of the column arrived and the Fascists fled, leaving numerous dead and wounded.

At dawn we slept for an hour or two in the station waiting-room at Lérida, where all other accommodation was occupied by the reserves, the supply column, and the hospital staff of the workers.

Towards midday, winding up the long mountain road from Fraga, we came out on to the top of the great plateau, which stretched as flat as a table for fifty miles or more before Saragossa.

Here we overtook the central column of the 'Army of Freedom,' under the command of Perez Farras, an officer of the regular army who has remained loyal to the democratic government, and Durruti, the well-known anarchist leader of Barcelona.

The column was an amazing sight. Every sort of vehicle, from Barcelona motor-buses and taxi-cabs to Rolls-Royce Limousines, was represented. Above them waved the flags of all the parties united in the struggle, the Republican flag of Spain, the flag of Catalonia, the red and black flag of the anarchists, and the hammer and sickle of the united Marxist parties now affiliated to the Communist International.

On the roof and along the sides of almost every car were red and white striped mattresses which the workers have brought with them from their homes, partly to sleep on by the roadsides, partly as a small protection against stray bullets.

The column is arranged in basic units of ten men, these again being organised in commands of 100 each. In front went fast cars to see that the road was clear, then followed the main part of the column in buses, lorries and requisitioned cars of every description, then came the petrol supply tanks and some distance in the rear a long line of Red Cross ambulances.

Near the head of the column I saw Caridad Mercadet, the white-haired woman member of the Political Bureau of the Communist Party, who had already distinguished herself nobly in the fight for the defence of Barcelona.

As the column moved slowly forward across the plateau, peasants, driving their sheep by the roadside, stood with their fists raised in the United Front salute, and in the villages, roads were lined with cheering people, who, a few hours before, had been hiding in the fields from the Fascist terrorists.

We advanced more slowly, keeping in touch by despatch riders with the other columns. Some wanted to dash straight forward to the attack at Saragossa, but Perez Farras and Durruti insisted that the assault must be co-ordinated with the other columns. For Saragossa is one of the strongest points in Spain from the strategic point of view, and a premature attack with insufficient forces might lead to a check.

Five hours of the afternoon we spent in a village, being fed in the houses of the peasants, who apologised for the fact that owing to the Fascist occupation they had been unable to feed their hens or to bring in vegetables or other crops.

Towards evening we advanced again and at dusk were going by the northernmost column of the three columns from Catalonia. With the head of the column occupying the next village, and the column itself stretching more than two miles along the highway, which is the Barcelona-Madrid main road, we halted for the night.

It was bitterly cold. In the car ahead of ours were three sergeants, two corporals and four privates from the regiment of sappers quartered at Barcelona.

These men had broken out of their barracks when the Fascist officers tried to force them to attack the workers of Barcelona, and had taken part in the fight on the side of the workers.

They had brought with them from the barracks a field telephone apparatus, trenching tools and the other useful implements.

They had thrown away their uniforms, and were now all dressed in the blue overalls of workers.

With their trenching tools they dug themselves a hole in the ditch at the side of the road, where they rolled themselves up in their mattresses against the cold.

We all ate dry bread and sardines, which are the ordinary ration of Spanish soldiers at the front.

By nine in the evening the columns were silent under the moon, with forked lightning playing over the high sierras to the north, and no sound to be heard but the loud buzzing of millions of grasshoppers rising over the plateau.

Between dawn and sunrise more bread and pieces of salami sausage were distributed.

After sunrise we heard the hum of an aeroplane far off. It was supposed that this was one of our own planes on a reconnaissance flight from Saragossa.

It circled above us. First a speck in the deep blue of the Spanish sky, then dropping lower.

We then saw that it was a foreign plane of some description. (We learnt later that the plane had been put at the disposal of the Fascists by one of the foreign commercial aviation companies already in Spain following negotiations with the Fascist governments in Berlin and Rome. Whether this particular plane was of German or Italian make I am unable to say.)

Suddenly, as we stood there, shading our eyes against the blazing sun and peering at the machine above, there came a swift whizzing sound, like the noise of silk being torn.

And a second later a violent explosion as a column of earth and smoke shot up from a point about 400 yards to the side and to the rear of our column.

Before we had time to throw ourselves flat on the road there came another and another.

Some men rolled swiftly to the ditch for cover. Others reached the cornfields by the roadside and lay flat among the wheat stacks.

I saw one man a few yards from me fall with blood streaming from his head.

In a few minutes Red Cross men were running down the column with stretchers. In this first attack there were two dead, including a woman, and six wounded.

The enemy plane circled high, again and again. We heard it coming up fast to the rear of the column.

One of the first bombs had broken the telegraph wires by the roadside, and engineers worked quickly to repair them, so that news could be got through to the temporary aeroplane bases at Lérida.

Owing to the fact that nothing had been known of the successful negotiations between the Saragossa Fascists and their friends abroad, the air attack had been quite unexpected.

By the time the second attack came most of the columns had had time to scatter into the fields 100 yards from the cars upon the high road.

With a vague idea that any cover is better than none, I ran in the direction of a couple of haycocks, I thought, 'Shall I take the one on the left, or the one on the right?'

A worker running beside me made for the one on the right. I followed him. Five seconds later I saw a bomb drop plumb into the one on the left.

The next fell 100 yards further on and a great cloud of acrid smoke hid the column from us as we lay flat, listening to the whistle and bang of the bombs falling all along the line.

None of the cars were hit, but there were some further casualties. The occupants of the Fascist plane returned to Saragossa and fifteen minutes later there were two of them over us with a new supply of bombs.

By this time the majority of the column had been able to reach fairly good cover several hundred yards from the road.

Again we lay flat as the enemy plane swooped over us dropping bombs every 200 yards or so along the line, and again failing to hit the roadway and the column.

A moment later the first of our own aeroplanes, piloted by Sandino, appeared, and ten minutes after that a big military plane from the base at Barcelona. The Fascists then made off.

The attack might have been expected to shake the nerve of this column of workers, most of whom have no experience whatever of this kind of warfare and have been trained only in the anarchistic technique of street fighting in Barcelona.

Yet that great column faced the situation with a most heroic discipline which will go down in the annals of the revolutionary struggles of the working class.

There was astonishment and, at the first, some confusion, regarding the proper measures to be taken. Then, under the orders of the commanders, the petrol tankers were manoeuvred out of the line and taken back to a point of safety, patrol cars and motorists were sent off along the road we had come, and, finally, a number of men were sent down to Lérida to take charge of the organisation of reinforcements.

We had the job of taking down to Lérida a Communist worker, who had been leader of a group of tanks which had suffered most in the attack; three of them had been blown to pieces.

He himself, a picture of grim, cold determination, was dashing down to Lérida to organise a new group and return that same afternoon to the battle front.

As we left, the column was being disposed along the road in a somewhat more open formation so as to reduce the danger of air attack during the wait which was still necessary in order to permit the other columns to reach striking distance.

It was the general opinion that the main purpose of the bombing of the columns, which served no other useful military object, was the hope of creating a panic which would result either in a withdrawal or in a too precipitate advance to the assault of the city.

In this objective the Fascists miserably failed, defeated by the grim heroism of the workers of Barcelona, who, having defeated the Fascists in their own streets, are now battling for freedom in the plains of Aragon.

Within Saragossa itself the general strike of the workers is absolute. Workers who escaped from that city and joined our columns reported that the place is like a city of the dead, with the Fascists in black shirts driving through the deserted streets, looking for men, who, at the point of the gun, they can compel to take part in the defence of the barracks against the advancing workers.

The Fascists are in occupation of the barracks on the hills above the town, also of the principal military and government buildings in the centre of the city, which makes an aerial bombardment of their positions very difficult.

They have shot the trade union leaders they have been able to find. Others are in hiding in order to assist advancing relief forces.

Daily Worker, 4 August 1936

1,000 WORKERS A DAY TRAINED IN MADRID

MADRID, Monday.

On reaching the capital yesterday I found the city calm and quiet – almost cheerful.

An heroic struggle is in progress on the sierras, fifty miles north of the city. Young militiamen drawn from Madrid's working class, are performing amazing feats of heroism, in face of Fascist machine-guns, planes and bombs. New militiamen are receiving a hurried training in the barracks here, prior to being sent north, where they are going at the rate of 1,000 a day.

Amid scenes of tremendous enthusiasm the city turned out

yesterday to receive a big contingent of troops from Valencia, marching through on their way to the northern front. The crowds greeted them with cheers, and the raised fist salute was given by all the throngs who lined the streets, with cries of 'Proletarian brothers, unite.'

A decree issued today deprives all ex-officers and other officials who have not yet declared their loyalty to the democratic government, of their pensions and other emoluments.

Fascist propaganda here and abroad is being directed to a desperate attempt to split the People's Front with sensational announcements of the revolutionary aims of the working-class parties. The Fascists hope by these means to detach the middle-class elements.

These attempts are failing miserably, in face of the clear announcement by the leaders of the Communist Party that they are wholeheartedly engaged in the defence of Democracy and the Republic.

The news has been received here with great enthusiasm that a People's Front government has been formed in Catalonia over the weekend on the widest possible basis of defence of the people against Fascism.

Three seats in the new Catalonian Cabinet are held by representatives of the United Socialist Party of Catalonia, recently formed by the merging of four hitherto existing working-class parties, the Communist Party of Catalonia, the Socialist Union, the Catalan Proletarian Federation and the Socialist Federation of Spanish Workers.

Daily Worker, 12 August 1936

FASCISTS CAN BE DEFEATED SAYS CABALLERO

MADRID, Tuesday.
After my return from the front this morning I interviewed Largo Caballero at the trade union headquarters.

He first of all asked me to convey, through the *Daily Worker*, the warmest thanks and appreciation of the Spanish trade unionists to all those British workers who have expressed sympathy and support for the struggle of the Spanish people. He mentioned particularly a telegram of support that had been received from the London Trades Council.

He pointed out that while resolutions and demonstrations of support are of tremendous value, practical aid can also be given by workers abroad by means of direct material assistance and by the exercise of great vigilance in preventing capitalist intervention on behalf of the Fascists against the Spanish Republic.

Caballero referred, as an example, to the offer of the famous 'Jimmy Collins' group of American airmen, who two days ago wired the *Mundo Obrero* offering their services free of charge to the Spanish People's Front.

'United action by all workers and other anti-fascists is essential,' declared Comrade Caballero. He asked me to re-emphasise the plea for unity he had made at the London meeting of the International Federation of Trade Unions.

'I have always felt certain', he said, 'that unity would be built against Fascism. Today the workers of Spain are fighting shoulder to shoulder, undivided on any party lines. This unity in action will lead to even closer unity as the practical result of our day-to-day struggle.'

This, said he, is 'the nation in arms against destruction, repression and reaction. The decisive stand taken by the workers from the very outset has been the determining factor of the Spanish struggle.'

Turning to me he continued, 'You yourself have been with me at the front and we have been together in the rear. You have seen for yourself the spirit of the workers, how our militiamen fight. You have stood with me in the fields of Castille and seen peasants – men, women and children – burning with the spirit of struggle.

Turning to the international aspect of the struggle, Comrade Caballero said the results of the workers' action would prevent the defeat of democracy throughout Europe.

'Fascism means not only oppression; it also means war,' he said earnestly.

Daily Worker, 13 August 1936

WITH MEN AND WOMEN FIGHTERS IN FRONT LINE

MADRID, Tuesday.

I spent last night with the front-line forces – the famous Mangada Column – at Novalperal, lying to the extreme left of the sierra front. Mangada himself was born in Cuba, and became a Colonel in the regular Spanish army. He is one of the very few high officers remaining loyal to the democratic government.

He told me with great pride that his column was composed almost exclusively of workers with a tiny sprinkling of regular officers and a few army machine-gunners. He told me of the terrible hardships and privations endured by these men in the first few days when supplies were poorly organised. Then they fought hungry under continual bombardment by Fascist planes.

Now, largely owing to the splendid work put in by the Special Sections of the Madrid Railwaymen's Committee, an excellent supply service is working well, with a full supply of cooks and field kitchens available.

The railwaymen at Madrid's northern stations have constructed special armoured trains – one of which is called the 16 February – which regularly patrol the line to Novalperal and beyond.

Women are also fighting with the Mangada Column. Mangada told me of the death of one young girl while advancing under heavy machine-gun fire to capture a neighbouring village.

The training of recruits is in full swing a few hundred yards behind the front line. Ammunition supplies are now sufficient to enable rifle practise to be carried out.

'Join the Fifth Regiment Fighting for a Free, Strong and Happy Spain,' is the slogan of a big militia recruiting campaign which is opening over the weekend with a magnificent display of posters and lavish leaflet distribution in all districts. The Fifth Regiment is composed entirely of workers.

Daily Worker, 15 August 1936

'I SAW NUNS QUIETLY SEWING'

Rich Blonde Wanted Militia To Cure Her Sister's Cold

MADRID, Friday.
'We wish to thank the militia for their kindness and the assistance they have given us, and to express both our gratitude and our admiration for the manner in which they have cared for the works of art and other valuables of this church. – Signed, Sister Veronica La Gasca.'

I held in my hands this morning a letter from which the above is an extract. I had just bought on a news-stand one of the few copies of British papers reaching here, in which it is stated that militiamen and other workers are committing outrageous actions against churches, priests and nuns.

I have seen only two previous copies of British papers during the last four weeks, therefore – despite one article seen in the *Daily Mail* – I had no conception of the character of the lies that are being told about men and women who are fighting here for elementary democratic rights and for the defence of the Spanish Republic.

Having read the British newspaper this morning I decided on an immediate test. I asked a Republican Guard standing by the news-stand to direct me to the nearest church. He showed me round a corner, where I found in the Plaza De Conde Toreno the church and convent of the 'Nuns of the Religious Order of the Capucines of the Most Immaculate Conception'.

I explained to the militiaman at the door that I wanted to see the church.

'There's nothing much to see here,' he said. 'We have sent the best pictures to a museum for fear that they might get damaged.' (Later I saw these pictures duly preserved in the museum.)

Saying that, nevertheless, I wanted to see the church, I went inside. In the dim interior I found twenty beds neatly made up, for this had been made the sleeping quarters of two militia sections.

Only two paintings were left on the walls. The militiaman pointed to these as copies or merely inferior paintings of little value and not worth taking to the museum.

The militiaman in charge had been for twenty years chief clerk looking after the foreign correspondence of a large British firm here. He told me the story of his church and convent.

During the first day's fighting three priests occupied the church and kept up a continuous sniping at workers in the street. By the time a force of militia, headed by my informant, arrived, the priests had fled, leaving twenty-one nuns in the convent bulding who had taken no part in the sniping.

The militia offered to set aside part of the convent for the use of the nuns and give them every protection. The nuns, headed by Sister Veronica La Gasca, said they preferred to go to the private houses of friends. A few days later Sister Veronica came back to see the church and, filled with amazement, wrote the letter of thanks and admiration which I have already quoted.

I found the letter lying with other papers on the table used as an office table by the militia commander. He did not regard it as a very important document, being unaware of the kind of lies that are being told about the people's militia abroad.

After examining the church I went through the convent, which has been turned into a women's prison, owing to the fact that the other prisons were full of male Fascists captured during the fighting in Madrid.

On the ground floor are women charged with theft and other non-political offences. The next floor is entirely occupied by women political prisoners who are in the rooms formerly used by nuns. This is the principal prison for women political offenders, having about 200 occupants. Many of the prisoners are nuns who were caught with arms in their hands or handing ammunition to priests firing at democrats and Republicans from the windows and roofs of churches.

I saw about 100 of these prisoners sitting quietly sewing. On a large, pleasant balcony running along the back of the building were a number of other political prisoners, most of them wealthy women found engaged in anti-Republican activity or concealing arms for Fascists in their bedrooms.

The balcony reminded me more than anything else of the sun deck of a liner. Well-dressed women, many wearing gold wrist watches and other valuables, were chatting, reading, rubbing their faces or legs with cold cream or adjusting their hair.

In a room opening on to a corridor sat the daughter of a Fascist marchioness, plucking her eyebrows before a mirror.

The marchioness herself – a bulky old lady in a black silk dress with a costly necklace round her neck – reclined in a comfortable chair. The third daughter – a blonde with an elaborate permanent wave – jumped up when we came in, complaining that her sister had a cold and could not the militia do something about it.

On the top floor of all, with a large expanse of roof to play on, are about thirty children of non-political women prisoners. The children are being looked after here until it is possible to find suitable accommodation for them elsewhere. I saw rows of little beds each painted with pictures from Walt Disney cartoons and other film characters, including Popeye, Betty Boop, Micky Mouse and the Three Little Pigs.

The children were singing and dancing outside in the sun. The nurse in charge of them – a well-known worker of the Communist-Socialist youth – complained bitterly that the accommodation was not really adequate because the beds were too close together. She also said the roof was dusty and required constant washing for fear the children should fall down and get dirt in cuts.

She explained that she was taking steps to get the militia to carry out the necessary structural alterations.

The militia leader grinned and admitted that the nurse had 'been after them' several times a day in order to hasten the improvement of the children's conditions. He had not, of course, heard of the atrocity stories being told in England against the democratic forces, but when I told him some of them he expressed the hope that the *Daily Worker* would now be able to give British readers the truth as witnessed by its correspondent.

Daily Worker, 26 August 1936

FIERCE FIGHTING ON THE ANDALUSIAN FRONT WITH THE DYNAMITERS

Epic Heroism Of Spanish Miners

PEDRO ARPAD (Southern Front), Tuesday. In blistering heat, among mountain rocks and vast undulating olive plantations, officers and men of the old army loyal to the government are fighting side by side with peasants from a hundred villages and miners from every pit in northern Andalusia. This front presents a terrific panorama of the united defence being put up by the Spanish people of their country and their Republic.

From the sun-scorched slopes of the Sierra Morena – a wild mountain range, formerly a famous haunt of bandits – I looked down yesterday across miles of olive trees to a point where the River Guadalquivir runs blazing in the sun under the Alcolea Bridge, which is the keypoint of the struggle to win back Córdoba and all Andalusia for Spain.

The bridge is defended by Moorish levies, hired, transported and commanded by traitor Spaniards with foreign assistance.* The levies are kept in hand only by promises of limitless looting.

Already proof has been found on the bodies of their dead that they are freely pillaging the works of art in the churches, which on Republican territory are guarded and transferred for the benefit of the people.

With the Moors are the Foreign Legion, which is composed mainly of hardened criminals who are kept in life-long isolation from the people, and trained purely as a band of killers.

The democratic ranks, on the other hand, represent a cross-section of all that is best and healthiest in the Spanish people. Prominent in the fighting are young artillery officers and other technicians of a higher grade of intelligence than the

* Cockburn refers here, and in subsequent despatches, to 'Moorish' troops when writing of the Nationalist Army of Africa. His tone reflects the conventions of popular journalism at the time.

average of the regular army officer.

A bearded young officer on the Sierra Morena said to me, 'What a pity the ground and trees prevent a clear view of the tactics and fighting qualities of our people. I assure you it is something beautiful to see.'

Another officer told the story of a democratic advance a few nights previously, which succeeded in capturing from the Fascists all the hamlets between the Sierra and Alcolea.

The Fascists had so manned the place with Moors and Legionaries that it appeared an absolutely impregnable nest of machine-guns. Ordinary attacks failed. It was death to approach within a mile of the place.

Then a miner from the mountains went to the officer in charge and suggested a plan. He said that neither the miners alone nor the regulars could capture the place. He therefore proposed to call for twenty-five volunteers from each to make a joint attack.

600 men in all volunteered for this desperate attempt. Fifty were chosen and under cover of the night they set out.

All the miners were picked 'dynamiters', highly-skilled workers, practised for years in using dynamite for blasting work at the mines. They carry belts full of cartridges of dynamite and have lighted cigars in their mouths from which to light the fuses at the proper time.

The soldiers, on the other hand, were all picked bayonet fighters. They crept through the olive groves together, slinking swiftly from tree to tree. The Fascists, heavily protected against ordinary rifle or machine-gun fire, had not reckoned on the dynamiters.

Daily Worker, 27 August 1936

'FASCISTS NO CHRISTIANS'

Catholic Leader Is For Popular Front

ALICANTE, Wednesday.
Hundreds of thousands of Catholic laymen have greeted with enthusiasm the nation-wide broadcast made by the famous

Catholic lawyer, ex-Cabinet Minister and former Governor of
Barcelona, Don Angel Ossorio y Gallardo.

Ossorio y Gallardo – who is probably the most eminent
Catholic layman in Spain – said that he thought it might be
useful to explain the position of all those Christians and
conservatives who are giving every possible support to the
Republican government.

'A Christian', he said, 'cannot be a Fascist because
Catholicism means liberty of spirit and respect for human
thought, whereas Fascism means the rule of force to protect a
privileged class.

'A Catholic cannot follow those teachings which demand the
extermination of the Communists and the Jews because the
Catholic doctrine demands that one should love one's enemies.
Even if liberals, Communists and the Jewish people were the
most abominable people on earth, a Catholic could still not
attempt to exterminate them.

'A Catholic should not tolerate the name of God being
invoked to attack the legitimate government of a country.

'A Catholic ought to respect and obey the Church, but a
Church inspired by the noblest teachings. Such a Church is not
to be confused with the church of bishops, loaded with jewels,
who bring the Holy Sacrament into play as an electoral and
political weapon against the Left parties. Nor is such a church to
be confused with those religious orders which hoard millions in
money and with clergy who desecrate the sacred character of
the churches by firing from them upon the people. Nor with
those who appear on the battlefield to shoot the defenders of
law.

'A good conservative', Don Angel declared, 'cannot attempt
to conserve oppression of a huge majority by a minority of
wealth, and must understand that the most substantially
conservative element is the people itself.

'A good conservative ought to remember what was said by
Pope Pius XI about the existence of that category of goods
which the state must almost reserve for itself by its own
economic power.

'A conservative must both refute the Fascist doctrines and
abominate the action of a political party which seeks power by
causing the state army to rebel against the state itself. A
conservative must be horrified by the unnecessary and incessant
crimes committed by the rebels, for if he is not, he cannot

condemn either any unnecessary reprisals on the other side.

'And here', he concluded, 'you have in a nutshell the reason why a man like me, a conservative and a Christian, find myself on the side of the government and the People's Front: for the Republic? Obviously! For Spain? Of course! But, above all, for other and higher motives, for genuine spiritual values, for self-determination of the people and the liberty of man.'

Daily Worker, 1 September 1936

MADRID RAIDER WAS FOREIGN

MADRID, Monday.

The population of Madrid is calmly preparing for further bombing attacks by Fascist raiders, having been put on the alert by the raid already described in the *Daily Worker*.

The bombing raid has been followed by another visit from a plane, which dropped leaflets bearing exaggerated claims of Fascist victories.

All Republicans and democrats are deeply outraged by the bombing of Madrid, an open town. Adding to their indignation is the fact that one of the raiders was a foreign plane piloted by a foreign airman. The plane was of a type which 'neutrality' regulations prohibit the government from acquiring.

From personal acquaintance with all the battle fronts of Spain, with the exception of the Asturias, where I have not yet been, I can state absolutely definitely that the democratic forces would by now have had the Fascists in full retreat but for the fact that the latter have been supplied with the very latest weapons of war by foreign powers.

While the British government is permitted to maintain its present attitude, gallant men and women are dying under bombing and shell-fire from foreign Fascists on all fronts.

For every moment which British democrats permit the National Government to maintain its present attitude scores of lives are being sacrificed to defend democracy throughout the world. These fronts are the frontiers of freedom, not only for Spain, but for Britain. Opposition to the supply of arms to the

Spanish government, on a 'neutrality' plea, is the grossest treachery, equivalent to loading bombs on the machines that are attacking Spanish fighters at the front.

The machine which flew over Madrid, dropping leaflets, was apparently attempting to spread panic among the population. The leaflet is a typical Fascist product with a map showing those sections of Spain which are alleged to be in the hands of the Fascists. Since only about half the territory claimed is really in their hands and everyone knows this, the map has probably done Franco and the Fascists more harm than good.

The text is a mixture of bombast, pleading and threats. With staggering impertinence this man, at the head of a horde of perjured generals and colonels, profiteers and land speculators, hired Moroccans and Foreign Legionaries, a man living on foreign money and having as his main armaments a fleet of foreign planes, calls on the capital of Spain to surrender to him.

Franco offers to be 'merciful' in the event of immediate surrender. Otherwise this 'patriot', who, with the financial assistance of Spain's worst foreign enemies, has bribed the biggest blackguards in North Africa to attack his native country, threatens to use his foreign planes to bomb the open city of Madrid.

If anything was needed to rouse the people of Madrid to the most energetic action against Fascists at the front and agents in the city this is it. The city itself is calm and totally undisturbed by the bombardment, but heartily indignant at the latest evidence of rebel savagery.

I have myself talked with men and women who a few days ago were not active, but are now demanding to know what they can do to wipe out these people. In the meantime art treasures in the famous Prado Gallery are being moved into cellars as a protection against possible destruction.

It is reported that stories are being sent from Valladolid through Lisbon joyously describing the 'destruction' caused in Madrid by the bombardment. I can only say that the bombardment was of such a character that I was unaware of its progress until I was roused from sleep by the sound of government anti-aircraft guns.

One of the planes shot down at the front a few days ago was not only a foreign plane but was piloted by a foreign Fascist. Deserters from the other side state that large numbers of foreign Fascist offices are active in the enemy ranks.

A battalion of the Foreign Legion on the sierra front has revolted and arrested its officers. The revolt was suppressed by the Fascists with great difficulty.

I was able to confirm this morning the frequent stories of discontent among ordinary regular army soldiers in the enemy ranks. There is a whole section of the sierra front where soldiers refuse to fire except when Fascist agents present pistols, threatening to shoot any man who refuses to obey orders.

It is actually possible to walk within 200 yards of the enemy lines and be greeted with shouts of 'Long live the Republic' from the lines.

Daily Worker, 4 September 1936

YOUNG BRITON, IN RIDDLED PLANE, FIGHTS FASCIST AIR TRIO

'The Fascist Crate Dropped Giddily, Burst Into Flames'

MADRID, Thursday.

John Wilson, twenty-one-year-old British student, who is lying wounded in the Military Hospital here, told the *Daily Worker* today the story of his amazing battle in the air, the petrol tank of his plane leaking, against three Fascist fighting planes.

Wilson left London a month ago with three pounds in his pocket determined to reach Spain by hook or by crook to take his place in the world front-line defence of democracy.

With extensive knowledge of aeronautical mechanics and considerable flying experience, he joined the Republican Air Force, and was stationed at Quatro Vientos aerodrome, in the Madrid province.

Last Friday afternoon, after a hard morning's work, he was just about to sign off, go for a wash and have a meal, when an emergency call came through to the aerodrome.

The Spanish pilot was all ready to take off the emergency plane, but was waiting for the machine-gunner who usually accompanied him.

To save delay, Wilson immediately volunteered to go up.

They took off and were flying, fairly high, towards their destination – which Wilson was naturally not allowed to divulge to me – when, out of the blue, there appeared three Fascist planes.

The game looked like being up when Wilson's smaller plane became caught in the Fascist air triangle – one plane above, one on either side, spitting out bullets.

At this point Wilson's right side was lacerated by an enemy bullet.

The Spanish pilot, still unhurt, swooped the plane down out of the triangle and, rising again, gave Wilson a chance to fire down on the outside enemy plane.

Wilson – blood pouring from his leg, his head reeling – looked down, saw the bullet-struck petrol tank leaking.

'I suddenly felt mad with rage,' said Wilson: 'all the hatred I ever had for Fascism boiled up in me. I let fly against the Fascist plane. The last thing I remember was the sight of the Fascist crate dropping giddily and then burst in flames. And there we were flying down, expecting to land in enemy territory ...'

How the Spanish pilot saved both their lives getting the damaged plane back over the enemy lines, making a brilliant landing in a field before the plane burst into flames, is regarded as nothing short of miraculous by aviators here.

The pilot, who was unwounded, got Wilson out of the crate just as the militia hurried upon the scene with a stretcher and took Wilson to the nearest field hospital, whence he was later taken to the Military Hospital here.

I talked with the tall, white-haired Republican surgeon, who was extremely satisfied with Wilson's progress.

Wilson himself was bright and cheery, bursting with questions about the progress of the civil war and hungry for news from England. His temperature is already nearly normal. His wound is painful, but fortunately his thighbone was untouched, so the leg is expected to heal rapidly.

He is extremely comfortable and well cared for in a private ward, learning Spanish from a buxom Spanish nurse whose four brothers are all at the front.

He is itching to be back 'on the job'. I heard him arranging to go out to the aerodrome to teach the many young recruits how to machine-gun.

Daily Worker, 4 September 1936

ENGLISH SCULPTRESS KILLED IN SPAIN

Confirmation has been received of the death of Felicia Browne, a member of the Communist Party in London, who joined the government forces on the outbreak of the Fascist revolt.

Comrade Browne was a sculptress and had been holidaying in Spain for a week when the Fascists struck their blow. As soon as she heard that women were being accepted into the militia she offered her services, and as she complied with the requirements of physical fitness she was speedily accepted.

At first she was disappointed at only being used for patrolling the streets of the city, but after a short period of training in machine-gunnery she was sent to the front.

She was killed in the Tardienta sector while taking part in a night operation, the objective of which was the dynamiting of a railway station. The dynamite party were noticed by a much stronger section of fascists, and in the ensuing scrap Comrade Browne was shot through the head. Her companions were unable to rescue her body.

An old friend of hers gave the following appreciation to a *Daily Worker* representative yesterday.

An Appreciation

Felicia Browne, a keen craftsman, studied sculpture and metal work at the Slade and at a technical school in Berlin. There she made friends who had good reason afterwards to be grateful for her loyalty.

She would share everything she had with those destitute refugees from the Nazi terror, who stayed at her cottage in Billericay.

She had a fine courageous and adventurous spirit; wanderlust took her alone into the remotest parts of Transylvania, where she could sleep in the open and exchange her wood carvings for food.

In a Ruthenian village the inhabitants, unused to foreigners, traced her by the smoke of her fire in the forest and in wild procession surged, shouting and singing round her, threatening to lynch her for a witch.

It is easy for those of us who knew her to imagine her rising to face them, blinded by the torchlight, and saying in halting Czech, 'What do you want?' in such a way that they must have known that if they had wanted anything that she could give it was theirs. They went away quietly, dominated by her resolute spirit.

In England she did her ordinary Party work, selling the *Daily Worker* at midnight at transport depots, canvassing, and so on. No matter how humble the task set her she carried it through with a characteristic thoroughness.

She had her own troubles, constant poverty and sickness, yet these never daunted her.

Felicia dies as she lived – a courageous fighter for the cause which she knew was that of all suffering and oppressed peoples.*

Daily Worker, 5 September 1936

THE ARMY IN OVERALLS DEFENCELESS?

HOW FASCIST ARMS SAVED THE REBELS

The seventh week of the war waged by international Fascism against Spain, its democracy and the simplest rights of its people is drawing to its close.

The sun sets tonight over nine battle-fronts, where a people is fighting for its country.

These nine fronts are the front-line defence of *your* democracy, *your* freedom, *your* peace.

The longest front is that which runs in a rough semi-circle

---

* This notice of Felicia Browne's death was the first obituary notice of a British volunteer to appear in the *Daily Worker*.

from the north-east of Madrid, beginning on the Saragossa road beyond Sigüenza and going through Somosierra, Guadarrama and Navalperal.

South and west of this front begins another – the Extremadura front.

This starts at a point north of the main Madrid-Caceres road, between Navalmoral de la Mata and Talavera de la Reina, runs in a wide curve near Guadalupe and Don Benito, and ends somewhere in Sierra del Pedroeo.

From there, south and east, runs the so-called Córdoba front. It goes along the south-western slopes of the Sierra Morena between Córdoba and Montoro, and bends round to encircle Córdoba between that city and Castro del Rio.

South of that front and entirely divided from it, the gallant, indefatigable people of Málaga maintain the amazing defence of their town against repeated attacks from Fascist columns. Málaga is an invaluable base for loyal ships moving along the south coast.

Around Granada democratic forces are at this moment in a position where an assault on the city may be expected hourly.

It is a far cry from there to the next fighting front around Teruel – territory seized by the Fascists in the first days of the military revolt and now completely surrounded by loyal forces.

In the north-east the democratic lines draw slowly closer to Saragossa and Huesca.

The eighth front in this list is that south of San Sebastián and Irún, where for a fortnight the Fascists have been hurling huge forces of troops against the defenders of this coastal strip.

Finally, on the Asturian front the miners of Asturias are avenging the long-drawn horrors of the end of 1934 and of 1935 in double action around Oviedo.

They are advancing against the completely surrounded city and at the same time are defending themselves against the repeated efforts of Fascist columns to raise the siege of Oviedo.

With the development of these fronts there has been a series of fairly well-marked phases in the character of the civil war.

The first phase – 18, 19, 20 and 21 July – consisted, of the wholesale betrayal of the country by the officers of the garrisons all over the country, seizure by them of all the arsenals and heavy guns, and an attempt to hammer the people of Spain into immediate submission to the will of this little group of brutal reactionaries and traitors.

They were for the most part swiftly defeated by people armed with old pistols and shot-guns, who rushed united into the streets determined to smash the Fascist attack or die in the attempt.

The next phase saw the democratic columns very hastily improvised – advancing to bottle up the Fascists in such centres as Saragossa, Huesca, Teruel, Granada, Córdoba. At the same time a terrific drive was made by the Fascist forces – particularly wealthy young Monarchists of Navarre and León and Burgos, with hordes of fanatical priests and soldiers driven forward at the revolver point to cross the Sierra Guadarrama, with the object of entering Madrid.

The first battalions of 'the army in overalls', rushing out from Madrid in lorries, buses and taxi-cabs, held the sierra in the face of the Fascist onslaught.

This was immediately followed by herculean efforts to organise a new 'People's Army' in the place of that other army which had deserted and attacked the people.

This was the period of the formation of the Fifth Regiment of militia based on a band of those who had already taken part in the first desperate struggle in the sierras.

Militias started getting military training, and the supply and quality of weapons improved beyond recognition as the workers of the rearguard factories got to work.

With the whole people – vanguard and rearguard – rushing on to a war footing against the enemy, it was obvious that nothing but a huge extension of international Fascist support for the rebels could save them from an immediate mopping-up, and prevent a swift end to the blood and horror of the civil war they had started.

As everyone knows, international Fascism flung its forces into the struggle against the people of Spain and democracy.

It is unnecessary to enumerate here the well-known evidence of a campaign which included both the supply of the first foreign Fascist aeroplanes to the rebels and an unprecedented campaign of lies against the Republican government and the democrats of Spain conducted in the Fascist and near-Fascist press of all countries.

This 'atrocity campaign' had the objective not merely of giving a free hand to international Fascist intervention, paralysing action by the government peoples, but also of covering up the appalling facts of Fascist terrorisation and slaughter in districts which – though nominally under their control – they feared they would be unable to hold except by actual physical elimination of the common people.

For the prolongation of war against democracy, foreign Fascist money, foreign Fascist planes, shells, bombs, rifles and machine-guns poured into North Africa and southern Spain.

With resources thus replenished, Generals Franco, Mola and Queipo de Llano conferred at Cadiz and raised a huge force of Moorish mercenaries by bribing the chiefs to send their men to what they supposed to be a new and easy conquest of a European empire.

Rushing these forces into Europe, they pushed northwards, committing in the march unspeakable outrages of which the wholesale massacre of innocent men and prisoners of war at Badajoz will remain for all time a black page in history.

The forces of the Republic, steeling themselves to a new effort, again met and broke the first rush of what had now become an international armed attack upon Spain, its people and its territory. The rebel generals' belief that they and their foreign allies would be able to sweep on to Madrid in a triumphal advance was shattered again, though the forces of this 'Black-Brown International' were able to establish contact with one another north and south along the line of the Portuguese border.

Then – in the middle of last week – they started throwing new material and forces into the fray.

All the previous ten days the railway line between Cadiz and Seville was choked with traffic taking aeroplanes of a 'certain power' up to the Seville military airport. Here they were being reassembled and fitted with bombs by foreign assistants also put at the disposal of Franco and Queipo de Llano by the same 'certain power'.

Daily Worker, 7 September 1936

FASCISTS RELY ON FOREIGN ARMS

Motley Throng Welded Into People's Army

MADRID, Sunday.

Visits to different fighting fronts during the past ten days have more than confirmed my view that the rebel forces have been receiving weapons after the signing of the so-called non-intervention pact.

They have conducted mass air attacks on most fronts, notably as accompaniment to push against Oropesa on road to Talavera.

Similarly there has been action all along western sector sierra front, where it was intended to make a push at Peñerinos simultaneously with a push on the road to Talavera, thus – as was hoped – squeezing Mangada column at Navalperal between pincer claws.

The rebels – believing that with resources of international Fascism suddenly thrown into play they will at last get the better of the militia – three times announced by radio that they had taken Talavera. This 'fact' was hastily spread about Madrid by Fascist agents, particularly those whose special business it is to keep in touch with foreign embassies and newspaper correspondents.

These same new forces, too, were those which enabled the rebels to detach a plane for an air raid on Madrid, intended by Franco not as a military manoeuvre but as an act of 'terrorisation'. To those who are unaware what the common people are capable of when fighting for the defence of their rights and liberties, the story of how this joint attack of the Fascist allies has been and is being met and repulsed – despite the cutting off of supplies of war material to the constitutional government by the operation of the Neutrality Pact – has seemed frankly miraculous. To those who have watched, as I have, the creation and development of the new People's Army, its achievement appears equally a miracle.

But it is a miracle not of chance or even simply of almost super-human courage and enthusiasm of these people.

It is rather a miracle of tireless energy and organising power devoted to canalising and directing the huge force of the people's will, enthusiasm, moral and physical strength so to make of it a force capable of meeting and beating the Fascist attack, thus creating out of the people itself a weapon, fit for the defence of the people by the people for the people.

The story of the creation of the Fifth Regiment of the militia – which, together with its fifteenth company being formed today is shortly to become a division – is too long to tell here with anything approaching adequacy.

This regiment is the backbone of the People's Army on fronts around Madrid and its steel companies and victory brigades have been active on other fronts, too.

In a magnificently furnished room, among gorgeous tapestries, pictures and carved bookcases full of rare volumes in costly bindings, I attended a few days ago a meeting of all the commanders of the companies of the Fifth Regiment from all sections of the sierra and Extremadura fronts.

There were present all ages, all trades. There were mechanics, chauffeurs, shopkeepers, bootmakers, bakers and barbers.

In overalls, with stars showing the rank to which they had been elected by the men under their command, with pistols and rifles, they had come straight from the battle front to take part in a conference.

Every man reported on the military, political and general situation on his section of the front. Each report was given briefly from notes scribbled while in the front line, then briefly discussed by all.

Problems which would have disconcerted and even appalled men of lesser character and ability or men fighting for a lesser cause, were described and dealt with in a spirit of cool objectivity and with a calm grasp of the whole situation – local, national and international – which frequently gave one an impression of being present at a meeting of leaders from some almost fabulous or legendary race of persons endowed with more than human qualities.

Yet a few short weeks ago these men were ordinary civilian citizens in Madrid, certainly playing a leading part in their trade unions, their sport organisations and in working for unity for all democrats and civilised persons against the Fascist menace which threatens all of us, giving every ounce of support to the constitutionally elected government of their country, but with scarcely a notion that before the summer had half gone they would be leaders of a People's Army on that 200-mile front where democracy faces Fascism, civilisation and progress face barbarism and reaction, and patriotic Spain faces the traitors.

The conference lasted three hours. At the close an earthenware pitcher of fresh water was passed round, together with a sandwich for each man before setting off again for the front.

Such meetings are being held all over the country all the time.

There have been important meetings of 'Rearguard Fighters', as for instance meetings of peasant committees guaranteeing the arrangement of constant food supply to fronts, hospitals and towns, meetings of women's committees to arrange the provision of homes for children of militiamen, orphans and refugee children from towns held by Fascists, and meetings to deal with arms, munitions, aeroplanes, clothing and factories, meetings of transport workers to discuss transport of food supplies and to ensure regular communications from one end of the country to the other.

In the rearguard, as in the vanguard, the fighting lines of the people of Spain march forward, united under one banner, united in the defence of the Republic, united in the determination that Fascism shall not win here.

Daily Worker, 8 September 1936

MADRID ACTS AGAINST GAS THREATS

MADRID, Monday.

The citizens of the capital read last night with their usual disciplined calm the instructions issued by the Mayor, and posted in all public places, in connection with possible Fascist gas attacks.

The Mayor has ordered all chemist shops to stay open day

and night, and has issued prescriptions for lotions to counter the effects of tear and other gases. The government, he declares, have accumulated chemicals for dealing with masses of gas which may be dropped. First-aid stations are being set up throughout the city.

The Seville radio has broadcast a report [carried in the more sensational British newspapers] that the world-renowned Calatrava Church, in the Alcalá, one of Madrid's most famous thoroughfares, has been turned into a dance-hall by the Communists. This report is as untrue as almost everything else that the Fascist General sends over the air.

I went to the church today and found it closed, guarded by an armed militiaman, with a notice on its front door, saying: 'This building is yours. Take care of it.'

Madrid's Communist men are at the front fighting, or in the factories ensuring maintenance of supplies. Its Communist women are some of them at the front too, if not fighting, nursing the wounded.

Others also are in the factories with their men-folk. Others are acting as militia in the town, looking after the children of those at the front, or of the refugees from Fascist territory. All are too busy to have much time for dancing.

In addition, the Communists respect the religious convictions of those thousands of honest Catholics who, seeing in Fascism a deathblow to all Christian ideals, are fighting alongside the Communists in defence of Republican democracy.

The Fascist announcer from Seville also broadcast on Friday night that Hendaye had been taken by their troops, apparently unaware that Hendaye was a French town.

Daily Worker, 9 September 1936

YORK HAMS FOR LOYALISTS

MADRID, Monday.
It is now a matter of hours how long the Fascists can still hold out against the loyal artillery's supreme attack on the Alcázar, Toledo.

An eye-witness reports that the two northern towers and the 18-foot thick northern wall has been completely demolished. Yesterday the south-western tower was destroyed by government artillery.*

Between two and three thousand people still in the Alcázar abandoned the main buildings and took refuge last night in vast subterranean network cellars as shells exploded in the central courtyard.

Answering a desperate appeal for food supplies from the Fascists, an enemy plane yesterday attempted to fly over with provisions. It got 'cold feet', however, and dropped the entire provisions, including 50 excellent York hams, half a mile from the Alcázar.

The local militia believe it may still be possible to rescue the wives and children of the workers and the loyal Civil Guards who are being held as hostages, providing they have not been murdered or left to die of starvation by Fascist officers.

The Week, No. 178, 9 September 1936

BODIES IN THE PARK

The gloomiest predictions of the outcome of events in Spain are now the stock in trade of the Foreign Office in their daily handouts to confidential journalists and interested persons. This gloom has its origin not in any examination of the military situation but in the messages of Mr Ogilvie-Forbes the special British representative, (see *The Week* No. 175).

Chief rumour set afloat last week by Ogilvie-Forbes was of the impending Madrid epidemic. Typhus, the Foreign Office explained was absolutely certain to sweep through the city owing to the 'dead bodies in the park', reported by the British representative to be 'arranged in piles'.

If Ogilvie-Forbes was the type of diplomat to make up wild stories the thing would be understandable, but he is not. On the

---

* The Alcázar is a fortress in Toledo that was besieged by Republican forces which never succeeded in capturing it.

other hand it has been definitely established that there are no bodies in the park, much to the disappointment of a photo-agency who on the Foreign Office tip sent a man post haste to photograph them. Indeed the only suggestion that there ever were any has been Ogilvie-Forbes's.

An example of the same thing appears in an account published yesterday by the London *Daily Herald* of their correspondent's trip to Madrid. After arrival he called on Ogilvie-Forbes who, in the words of the correspondent, was 'astounded' that a foreigner should be able to get to the capital.

It is peculiar, to say the least of it, that the British government representative in charge of evacuating the British should not know that foreigners can still travel by train.

Reports from Madrid suggest that the explanation is that Ogilvie-Forbes is now completely in the hands of alarmists and anti-government propagandists with whom he was on terms of personal friendship previous to the present civil war. It is they who supply him with these fantastic tales which some of them perhaps genuinely believe.

Daily Worker, 15 September 1936

FASCISTS WILL USE POISON GAS

MADRID, Sunday (delayed). British residents in Madrid were summoned to attend for gas drill instruction on Friday evening.

Ogilvie-Forbes, the British Chargé d'Affaires, has informed Britishers at the Embassy that he has definite information that the Fascists are going to use gas.

He gave this as a reason for first, sending out of Madrid all the last remaining Britishers possible; secondly, for providing gas-masks for the 150 Britishers bound to remain in Madrid.

Thus Forbes, who certainly cannot be accused of hostility to the Fascists or friendship for the government, is the first to admit that the Fascists are going to begin gas warfare. The only snag is that Forbes, apparently worried that the Britishers will be tempted to sell their masks for fabulous prices, is keeping all the masks in the Embassy.

Thus, if a British subject should happen to live in a suburb he will have a good half an hour's run to the Embassy to get a mask should a gas attack take place.

A further indication of the intentions of the Fascists is the fact that every soldier taken prisoner by the government forces last week was equipped with a gas-mask.

The urgency of the need for sending gas-masks to the Spanish people – already deprived of the elementary facilities for ending the war by the blockade of the 'neutral' governments – is too bitterly obvious to need emphasis.

Daily Worker, 24 September 1936

ALL ABLE-BODIED PERSONS CALLED TO GO TO FRONT IN DEFENCE OF MADRID

Rebel Treason Revealed

MADRID, Wednesday.
Following successes by the government forces at the besieged Alcázar of Toledo, a manifesto has been issued, signed by the leaders of all the parties of the Popular Front, calling upon all able-bodied people to join the People's Militia and go to the front.

The manifesto declares that this is the decisive moment of the struggle in Spain.

'For two months,' it says, 'the Spanish people have shown boundless heroism on the battlefields, and have covered themselves with glory as befits their tradition.

'At the walls of the enemy forts and on the steep slopes of the Guadarrama, our people have shown the world that they will never be enslaved, that the people of Spain can gain their liberty by force of the arms they bear.

'Madrid shall be the tomb of Fascism. The fight is near its

end, but the moment is grave.

'We must form a front of steel against the enemy.

'All able-bodied men to the front!

'Rather will we stand and die than live for ever on our knees to the enemy!'

This, Spanish government leaders have told a British delegation recently returned from Spain, is the position that the democratic countries of Europe will have to face if the Fascist rebels win the civil war.

The rebels have no money and they need arms. Germany and Italy have the arms and they desire certain strategic points possessed by Spain. So the bargain has been struck and, declare government leaders, formally embodied in a secret treaty signed some time ago.

The effect of this on the position of Britain and France is not easily calculable. What is obvious is not only that the Spanish Fascists are willing to trade for Italian and German help large portions of the country they have already betrayed, but that also the British National Government, by upholding a policy of neutrality, is pursuing a course directly contrary to its frequently stated policy of guarding British communications in the Mediterranean.

The delegation was able to gather many proofs from government leaders and from its own observation that while the present arms embargo against the government is maintained the rebels have every possible technical advantage on their side, for arms supplies to the Fascists are now even more frequent than they were before the embargo was imposed.

The delegation, consisting of William Dobbie, MP, Seymour Cocks, MP, Isabel Brown, secretary of the Relief Committee for the Victims of War and Fascism, and Viscount Hastings, went to Spain for the purpose of investigating conditions there, and interviewed not only trade union leaders and workers, but also Azaña, President of the Republic; Caballero, Prime Minister; Prieto, Minister of Air and Marine, and other prominent members of the government.

The treaty was referred to particularly by Prieto, Mr Seymour Cocks told a gathering of pressmen yesterday, but it was also mentioned by Caballero, and was known to the whole of the government.

Mr Cocks said Prieto had reminded the delegation that Spain had always acquiesced in the control of Gibraltar by Britain, but now the Spanish Fascists were not only declaring that they would demand the cession of Gibraltar, but it was known that there was in existence a treaty by which, in return for arms, Italy would be given the Balearic Isles and Germany would receive the Azores as a naval base in the Atlantic.

The Azores are a Portuguese possession, but Portugal will be given in compensation the Spanish province of Galica.

Prieto pointed out that such a bargain would have a very grave effect on Britain's position in the Mediterranean.

In another interview Largo Caballero also spoke of the fact that the rebels had promised Spanish possessions to Germany and Italy in exchange for arms, and said that Couta had been promised to Germany.

A significant fact, in view of the recent British Trades Union Congress decision on neutrality, is that the acting president of the Spanish TUC told the delegation that the trade union movement was extremely disappointed by the British decision to adopt a non-interventionist policy. He denied that the Spanish movement had ever declared itself in favour of a non-interventionist policy.

The impressions of the delegation, placed before Díaz Alor, acting president of the Spanish TUC, and confirmed as correct by him, were as follows:

1) That the Spanish people feel disappointed at the attitude of neutrality adopted by the democratic countries. 2) That they cannot agree to the rebels being accepted by any country on a basis of equality with the popularly elected government of the country. 3) That since the imposition of the neutrality agreement there seems to have been a more rapid importation of arms than before on behalf of the rebels.

4) That the people of Spain demand the rights of the government to purchase in markets material to defend the state. 5) That under international law they have the right to purchase arms, and that they deplore the attitude of democratic governments in arriving at decisions which can only help the Fascist rebels in the struggle and act against the forces of democracy not only in Spain, but all over the world.'

A statement read by Mr Dobbie said that representatives of the delegation spent a night and a day with a machine-gun crew. The delegation had with it a bomb dropped from a plane which was supposed to be a passenger plane and had made a forced landing. The whole construction of the plane was that of a fighting machine, and there was no room for passengers in it.

Another 'exhibit' was a parachute used by an Italian airman when his plane crashed, and a statement made by the airman.

'The policy of so-called neutrality is an absurd fake,' Caballero told the delegation. 'It is only helping the rebels, who are continuing to get help from Fascist governments.

'The right policy is to give the legal government of Spain all the help to which it is entitled, and the right to buy arms.'

Caballero said the government needed arms to equip an army of 200,000 men, and if they could obtain those arms they would win very quickly. They also wanted aeroplanes and ammunition. The government would fight to the end and would win, but as long as the rebels were being supplied with arms the end would be delayed.

Daily Worker, 25 September 1936

'THEY HAVE NEW BOMBS, NEW PLANES'

Rebels Get Constant German Aid: Loyalists Drill With Sticks

The Steel Battalion of the Fifth Regiment is the backbone of the Spanish people's fight for democracy. I was a militiaman in that battalion.

This is not an analysis of the situation in Spain. It is the first-hand story of what actually happens on the front where the forces of democracy and freedom meet the forces of international Fascism.

As a touring journalist in a motor car you stand a good chance to be killed, but you don't necessarily see what happened any better for all that. As a private in the front line you see things you can't see any other way.

In these articles I am telling you simply what I saw. The conclusions you can draw for yourself.

In early September we moved into position on the sierra. The days were quiet, but getting colder. The shells of the heavy guns sang to and fro overhead at night and rifle bullets ripped through the trees and sometimes fell into our kitchen.

But if you kept under cover by day and at night, remembered not to sit up suddenly in your sleep so as to put your head into the path of a bullet you were safe enough and even comfortable.

Then there began to be rumours. Rumours drifted up and down the sierra and up north from the Talavera front. Rumour said a new rebel pincer drive on Madrid had begun. Something bigger and worse than anything we had seen yet, and what their attacks were like.

They had got still more planes. How many? Nobody on the front knew exactly at the time, though we knew later. All we knew was they had upwards of twenty more of them, brand new Junkers, with German pilots, making somewhere near ninety with the ones they had already.

The new ones had come in within the past three weeks, brought across the Portuguese frontier, assembled in Spain and now ready for action.

Still, for a day or two nothing much happened, barring the rumours, and every now and then a wounded man passing through our position with a grim story of the new Junkers.

One night the little sergeant – four weeks ago he was a butcher's boy down in Aranjuez, the Elstree of Spain – crawled puffing and careful through the boulders, edged between two perpendicular rocks, and lowered himself on to the ledge where I squatted on guard.

He handed me a stoutish twig, quarter of an inch thick and six inches long. He explained that next time the bombers came over I had to put the twig between my teeth and hold it there, at the same time gripping my head between my hands, and lying flat as we had learned to do already.

I said I was no acrobat and what was the big idea anyway? He laughed. 'All the same,' he said, 'This is pretty serious. You see they've got new aeroplanes – Germans – and new bombs – Germans, too. The old bombs were nothing. You lay still and if it didn't drop just on top of you, why you were perfectly safe.

'These new ones are different. High explosive. They drop somewhere near you and you get a shock that's liable to send you off your chump – shell-shock. Gripping your head that way and holding something between your teeth is supposed to be good against it. I don't know.'

I took the twig gingerly, stuffed it in the pocket of my uniform, and thought about the realities of non-intervention.

From the ledge where I was uncomfortably propped, with a

1914 Oviedo rifle and fifteen rounds of ammunition, you could see far out over the whole Guadarrama front and way up north-westward to where the mountain peak by Somosierra towered up into the evening sky.

Looking across that front I could not help remembering the words of Pericles in his famous funeral oration. 'We have no need of monuments to heroes. Our whole land is a grave and a monument of heroes.'

Not a square mile of that land below us that had not been fought upon, died upon, by the men who in the very first days of the Fascist attack had rushed out with pistols and sporting guns and in close-range fighting, and hand-to-hand fighting, barred the path to Madrid to the whole Spanish army with all its generals and horse, foot and artillery.

Looking up at Somosierra I thought of my friend Carlos San Martín, an out-of-work telephonist from Asturias, whose uncle was a Socialist councillor at Oviedo and had been murdered by the Fascists in the first hours of the rising there.

Carlos was one of the first few hundred who, as soon as the fighting was over in Madrid, went dashing out to meet the Fascist drive on the sierra. He drove a lorry with twenty-five others in it hell-for-leather across the plain I was now overlooking, and up the steeply winding road to Somosierra.

The officer in command of the forces hastily mobilised there gave the order to retreat – it was afterwards found that he had been in hourly communication with the enemy by telephone and he got shot for it.

But Carlos and his friends fortunately refused, at first at any rate, to obey his frantic efforts to hold them back. They got right up to Somosierra, and for seven hours they were cut off with 300 Fascist troops in front of them and another couple of hundred behind.

That was fighting in which absolutely nothing counted but personal courage, determination and drive.

In seven hours' fighting twenty-five bare-footed, hungry men sent those 500 soldiers – officered by professionals – scuttling back to positions prepared for them long months before, when Gil Robles was Minister of War, and the Fascists used the annual manoeuvres to lay the foundations of the deeply plotted betrayals of their country.

Carlos's exploit and all the hundreds of similar achievements that went with it in those days of late July seemed a long time ago now. For that was all in the days before 'non-intervention' clamped down its blockade against the democrats, and held the huge doorway of the Portuguese frontier wide open to the guns, shells, tanks, machine-guns and – above all – the aeroplanes that ever since had been pouring through it from the arms factories of the Rhineland and central Germany and northern Italy.

We were soon to learn just how much water had passed under the international bridges from the days of at least relatively equal combat to this day of mid-September when thousands of men found themselves facing with old rifles and not too much ammunition the attack of a full fleet of the newest bombing planes in the world.

We had seen something of it already back in the big barracks on Francisco Rodríguez Street where we did our training.

The place used to be the church and monastery school of the Salesians. It is ugly and new and has no works of art worth reporting on, so you will find no mention of it in the Madrid guide books.

In the history books of the future, on the other hand, it will have its page, for it was one of the nerve centres of Spain's fight for freedom, headquarters of the Fifth Regiment of militia.

When I was a child I saw Northumberland miners who had joined Kitchener's First Army, drilling with broomsticks in the fields at Berkhamsted. In Francisco Rodríguez Street I saw men tearing planks from a neighbouring ruin with their bare hands, and trying to break them into something approximately of equal length and weight to a rifle, so as to have something to train with.

Every morning when the just-risen sun was still throwing long shadows across the barrack square, and the women of Cuatro Caminos were queuing up at the foodshops in the street outside, the men of our platoon, who had all been enlisted together a few days before, used to gather round the half-dozen professional sergeants and officers we had there and ask, 'Shall we get rifles today?'

And they would say, 'Perhaps this evening. Perhaps to-morrow. In the meantime ...'

So in the meantime, with the crucial hours sliding past, and gentlemen in London and Paris arguing that 'non-intervention is what the Spanish people really want,' we marched and counter-marched, and practised moving in extended formation, with never a rifle among the lot of us.

There was a big peasant lad from Albacete, who had a fine voice and used to sing and dance sometimes for the platoon. One blazing afternoon, when for the twentieth time we had hung around the armoury waiting for rifles, they handed us out some dummy rifles to drill with.

He snatched his, thinking it was the real thing at last. Then he saw what it was. The new disappointment was too much for him.

I can see him now, standing with the dummy held above his head and the tears running hotly down his bronze cheeks. 'I want to fight, I want to fight, I want to fight for my country, and you give me this.'

And turning slowly on his heels, a full circle, calling to all four corners of the barrack square, he shouted, 'Why? Why? Why?'

I did not, as an Englishman, think it a suitable moment to tell him that there were certain of my countrymen who were at that very moment engaged in telling the men and women of England that non-intervention is working out all right.

After days of time wasted through the fault of nobody except of those who held up the supply of rifles to the democratic troops, we had moved up to the front.

In the platoon I was in there were eighteen men besides the sergeant: six peasants from south of Madrid, a young carpenter from Ciudad Real district, whose father had been executed by the Fascists in 1935 for the crime of being an alleged Socialist, two clerks from Toledo, a commercial traveller who worked for a chain-library organisation, three mechanics and a barber from Madrid, a brushmaker from Talavera, a bootmaker who had spent five weeks tramping across country to join up, a sixteen-year-old boy from Valencia, who had been a delivery boy, and myself.

Standing packed like sardines in a score of lorries we and the other men of the regiment's new companies jolted out of the barrack square one windy afternoon into the street where the workers of Cuatro Caminos were gathered in a vast cheering, flag-waving, singing multitude to see us off.

Women tossed huge green watermelons from their fruit barrels into the lorries to slake our thirst on the journey. Men surged round the lorries, roaring out their last 'Good-bye and good luck'.

Then Pedro Sánchez, a tough, fair-haired, blue-eyed peasant boy from Albacete, climbed on to the side of our lorry, and raising a voice like a bull's roar above the din, shouted what might stand as the slogan of the men who are fighting for Spain, and for a good life for themselves:

'Long Live the Spanish Republic!

'Long Live Democracy!

'Long Live the People's Army!

'Long Live Me!'

After a couple of hours driving and seven hours marching in cord-soled sandals over long mountain detours out of reach of the Fascists' heavy guns, and as far as possible under cover from the scouting aeroplanes, we reached our position, a stony hilltop high above the Guadarrama plain, forming an angle of the sierra front.

The two platoons who had held it before us for a month and whom we had now come to relieve, knew nothing as yet of the new arms that had come to the enemy from Portugal, and told us that the position was a very good one, easy to defend.

On equal terms it would have been. It was high up, and on three of its four sides it was possible to get a fairly commanding view of the approaches to it. On the fourth the pine trees grew thicker.

Our predecessors had built stone parapets around the edge of the position, excellent against rifle fire, and had constructed a score of little dwellings – half-hut and half-burrow – where you could lie comfortably out of the wind and out of reach of the bullets which sometimes zipped through the pine branches laid across to form the roof.

But all that was done in the days when the Spanish people did not yet know how deeply and how cruelly it had been betrayed.

On the night the sergeant gave me that sinister little bit of wood which was supposed to safeguard one against shell-shock, I came on guard at seven in the evening and went on again at two in the morning until seven.

Ordinarily there would then have been coffee and bread and several hours sleep.

But between dawn and sunrise we on guard knew already that something new was happening, and guessed that the pincer attack had at last begun. Out of the morning sky from the north we saw a fleet of planes flying high southward. As they came nearer we recognised them as the Junkers planes, of which we had already seen a few on one front or another.

A few minutes later we heard the first big bombs falling on the

positions held by the other sections of our company on higher
hills above us on our left.

Even at that distance we could tell that these were bigger,
deadlier bombs than the enemy had been using hitherto.

Sometimes they fell nearer to our position, and we could hear
them scream through the air, and see the earth and smoke, and
sometimes whole saplings, shoot into the air as they hit.

The pine woods began to burn, and long drifts of acrid smoke
swirled slowly across our position.

The bombing went on and on, each plane going off
northwards in turn to reload with Hitler's latest engines of death.
In the woods afterwards we picked up several unexploded
bombs, and portions of other bombs, all neatly ascribed with the
marks of the German firm which made them, thus setting at rest
any doubts any of us may have had as to just what
'non-intervention' means.

Then came two prisoners from the Fascist lines with a story
which confirmed everything we had heard.

They told us the Fascists, who had been gloomy enough
about their prospects hitherto, were perking up, because they
knew that they were not to be asked to attack again except
under the cover of a terrific barrage by the German planes.

'These German pilots are pretty good,' they told us. We asked
if they knew that all the pilots were German. They said all the
pilots and the machine-gunners were German, but that each
plane carried a Spaniard on board as a sort of sop to the pride of
the Spanish Fascist aviation officers.

They were in no doubt that the German planes and the
German pilots would do the trick.

When the bombing ended, the heavy shelling began; also
partially with German guns and German shells.

Then the planes returned, bombed, swooped low, and began
close range machine-gun fire.

We could see them circling low above the woods on our left,
and we thought of our comrades up there, with their old Oviedo
rifles like ours, their two machine-guns, their little ammunition.
We did not have to think long.

As my guard duty was coming to an end, I saw the first
evidence of the effects of the German bombardment. Slowly up
the hill towards us came three of our men, their faces blackened
from the bombardment and the burning, two of them with blood
oozing through dirty handkerchiefs tied around their wounds,

and carrying between them a fourth man whom I had known very well in the barracks.

I saw that the bottom of his face had been literally blown off, and that as his body sagged between the bearers, blood oozed horribly from the small of his back.

Bleeding, and stone deaf from the bombardment, they approached the position. When they reached it we saw that the man they were carrying was already dead.

They were all dazed. One of them said, 'But what are our planes doing?' Nobody answered.

We all knew that until London and Paris lifted their ban we should get no succour from those few gallant loyal airmen, who, outnumbered twelve to one by the German Junkers, were putting up an heroic and desperate fight on a half-dozen fronts at once.

Our position had suddenly become one of the most critical points on the whole sierra front, and one of the two or three key points in the whole defence of Madrid.

We who had just finished our guard were given an hour and a half to sleep, and a hunk of dry bread with a chunk of pork fat to keep us going (the water supply and the kitchen were both by this time under machine-gun fire, so there was no coffee and no stew).

We went on guard again before ten, and as the men in retreat from the positions on the left poured down the valley, and we heard the continuous whine of shells now dropping on our positions further to the rear of our own old positions, we all knew very well that the situation was about as serious as it could be.

I asked a sergeant what we were going to do about it. He shrugged and spat. 'Stay here. We've got to die some day.'

In this spirit opened a grim 36 hours. The story of that next tense day, night, and day I will tell in tomorrow's *Daily Worker*.

Daily Worker, 26 September 1936

BLOWN TO BITS BY A NAZI BOMB

For the first half of that morning we sat on our hilltop among the burning pines and the pitiable parapets, watching the men wounded by the German bombs being carried down the valley.

By midday our total numbers in that crucial outpost and angle of the sierra line had risen to seventy-two.

There were thirty-eight of our own two platoons, which had been together since the first day we enlisted back in Francisco Rodríguez Street, twenty-two men from the shattered company on our left sent over to join us, and twenty-two Assault Guards, who had been sent up the line as reinforcements.

They were magnificent fighting men. And they had an average of eight rounds of ammunition per man – the ration permitted to these defenders of democracy's front line by the powers that be in London and in Paris.

At one in the afternoon word was sent round the little encampment that all but the essential guards were to assemble in the angle of the central open space between the rocks and the pines and there listen to and discuss a statement that would be made by the Captain.

It was an impressive sight. Three score men or so, in their khaki uniforms, with thin bed blankets thrown like capes over their shoulders against the bitter cold, sat pressed close under the parapets and the rocks, with the bullets from the position above us on the left whining almost continuously close above their heads.

In the centre sat the Captain, a tall lame man of thirty or so, who had done ten years' service in the Foreign Legion.

When everyone was assembled and listening, he spoke as follows: 'Comrades, you all know that the positions which yesterday made this position a quiet one are now in the hands of the enemy. You all know why. The enemy has received a large consignment of German airplanes, the pilots are German, and there is no use pretending that these are not an exceedingly formidable force.

'As I have told you before, the position we hold here would be impregnable against infantry and machine-gun attack, even though we have no machine-gun.

'In the face of an aviation attack, such as our comrades suffered yesterday, the position is considerably more delicate. There may be some who will state that it is hopeless.

'The facts are, however, that if we take as good cover as possible during the air attack and are then, without demoralisation or delay, ready to rush from our cover to meet the attack of the infantry, we can certainly very seriously delay the capture of this position.

'To do this is essential, even at the cost of our lives, because every hour of delay here will give a further opportunity to the strengthening of the positions behind us between here and Madrid.

'We must not shut our eyes', he continued, 'to the fact that in this struggle against the forces of international Fascism which you see daily in the air above you, we may be called upon to die tonight or tomorrow morning.

'I would remind you comrades that every one of us will die sooner or later, and, as for me, I think it preferable to die fighting here tomorrow than to await a cowardly death in the future.

'I shall take the necessary military decisions in consultation with our comrade, the Lieutenant of the Assault Guards. But it is for you to discuss and comment upon the statement I have just made. If there are any here who are unprepared to accept the situation as I have simply and unexaggeratedly described it, let them go at once, leaving here their rifles, their ammunition, and their union cards. I have spoken.'

One man then leaned forward and asked a question about the actual destructive force of the new German bombs. Another inquired what were the possibilities of reinforcements reaching us that day, and was told frankly there was no such possibility.

A third man said that he had heard talk among three or four comrades to the effect that the position was hopeless, the Captain madly reckless, the place little better than a slaughterhouse. He had heard these comrades stating they would prefer to go to another position, join another company.

'Will the comrades referred to now speak,' said the Captain.

A boy got up and admitted that he had made such remarks. He said that as a member of the People's Army he claimed the right to state his point of view and to ascertain the feeling of all present.

'Certainly,' said the Captain, 'you have that right, and the comrades present have the right to decide as between you and me.'

The boy then spoke at length.

At least, he said, he and his comrades from the same village would prefer to be with another column in which, as they knew, most of the men from that village were serving. He also repeated what he had said about the foolhardiness of the Captain and the certain death which awaited all who might remain in our position.

'As for me,' he said, 'I am a practical fighter for freedom, and I do not consider it a good work for our country simply to commit suicide here in this spot.'

There was further discussion.

One man then asked whether, in view of the fact that the League of Nations was about to meet, according at any rate to the newspapers, it might be expected that by holding this position we could delay the advance of the enemy 'until the democratic powers have time to equal things up a bit'.

Following further discussion along these lines, I was then asked to state what might be the situation in Britain, and to estimate the possibilities of the British people being able to break down the ban on arms for the people of Spain.

I did so as well as I could, stating, I believe truthfully, that I could give the assurance that every hour we could hold out, even at the cost of our lives, would not be wasted, for our friends in England would use every one of those hours to the very full to help the people of Spain.

The discussion was then closed.

'Those', said the Captain, 'who wish to stay here with me will now move over to that side of the square. Those who agree with our comrade from Talavera district, and who wish to leave us will remain where they are.'

We all moved over, except for three men, who remained where they were.

The one who had spoken before then made a further brief speech across the intervening space, his words interrupted now by the continual whine and crash of heavy shell fire, stating that he must hold to his decision that from the point of view of the practical struggle to remain here was ludicrous and disastrous, but that he wished to make clear that he and his comrades had no intention of deserting, being on the contrary determined simply to move to another column.

They then deposited their arms, ammunition and cards on the burned grass and left the camp.

We went on guard again.

The wind rose and it became bitterly cold. It was rumoured that the air attack would begin at half-past five. At twenty minutes past five we on guard saw the Junkers squadron winging up from the north.

Word flashed round the camp.

The bare essential of guards was kept in position, where we

wedged ourselves as well as possible under the shelter of the big rocks. The rest were ordered to scatter as far as possible within the little encampment, lying flat, and if possible under the protection of rocks and boulders with which the place was littered.

Hidden, crouching like that, you are out of sight of all others, and you feel extremely lonely, with nothing filling the world except the increasing menacing hum of the advancing planes.

It was a serious test of the morale and the staying power of these lads from the farms and the workshops, whose total military training amounted to a matter of fourteen days, and many of whom had never seen an aeroplane three weeks ago.

A few minutes passed, and then came the scream of the first German bomb. It fell just outside the encampment, setting the pinewoods alight again. The scream and smash of the bombs seemed to tear the air apart and all the boulders shook as they fell.

In a couple of seconds between the falling of the bombs, I began to be able to hear the low cries and occasional moan of wounded men. In the first few minutes Pedro Sánchez, the man who a few days before had cried 'Long Live Me!' from the lorry as we left Francisco Rodríguez Street, was torn to pieces by a bomb.

He did not, after all, live long (he was only eighteen years old), but he died a very glorious death for the Republic.

There was a pause in the bombing, and for a moment we thought the Germans were gone. Then we heard them sweep lower, and we knew that the machine-guns were coming into action.

For a few ghastly minutes we lay there, hearing the savage roar of the planes close above us, and the continual loud cracking of the machine-gun bullets as they struck the rocks all about us.

There was nothing whatever to do except sit tight, get ready to jump from cover to meet an infantry attack so soon as the plane machine-gunning stopped, and in the meantime reflect on the curious workings of a world in which the democratic peoples permit their front line fighters to lie under rocks armed with old rifles, while allowing the bitterest enemies of democracy the latest weapons of modern warfare.

The rush from cover when the machine-gunning stopped was a fairly creditable performance. But there was, after all, no infantry attack that day.

Something had gone wrong, some of our militia had made a skirmish against the Fascist positions on the left, and instead of following up the air attack as they should have done, they preferred not to move down the hill.

The sun went down, and the quick southern darkness came over us. The cold grew worse. We were dog tired. It was arranged that half of those present should now sleep, keeping on their full equipment, and that the others should stand guard until midnight.

We crawled into our burrows and fell instantly asleep.

Quarter of an hour later the sergeants were running from burrow to burrow turning us out. Everyone was to form up immediately in the central open space.

The cold was worse than ever, the wind cutting through you in stabbing gusts.

In a moment the word was whispered round the forming ranks that we were to make a night attack on the high enemy position two miles away on the peak of the hill above us.

In quick, crisp whispers, the Captain explained the situation. 'So long as it is an equal fight,' he said, 'we are more than equal to them, even though they have twice or three times our number, as we know, I tell you frankly, they have.

'But we are fighting for freedom and they are not, and therefore we have the advantage of a great cause and a great spirit. We must, therefore, take every opportunity of engaging them when the fight is relatively equal, that is to say, when they cannot use the German planes.

'Tomorrow morning, if we do not attack now, the planes will come again. This time the infantry will come, and we risk being killed without delaying them more than half an hour or so. We shall, therefore, attack now. Move on.'

In silence broken by the constant noise of men falling down among the thorns and rough boulders of the tiny mountain track we moved out of camp, down our side of the ravine between us and the enemy mountain, and began the long climb towards the summit, where the Fascists lay entrenched.

We knew that they had a quantity of German machine-guns and machine-rifles, but we thought it probable that even if with nothing but rifles we were unable actually to storm the position, we should probably scare them into abandoning all plans for attack on the following day. This, in fact, is what happened.

After a long and agonising climb through the rocks we came to the edge of a gently sloping open space stretching a hundred and fifty yards or a little less up to the enemy position. There were small boulders and a few pine trees.

Crawling cautiously, we advanced to within a hundred yards of the position. There was complete silence except for the noise of the heavy shells passing across our heads in an artillery duel between forces on our left and right.

For a matter of fifteen minutes we lay there among the rocks.

Finally, after hurried whispered discussion, we agreed that the time had come to test the enemy position. We were so near that we could plainly hear their footfalls, and the voices of their guards talking to one another.

We fired two shots and waited.

There were a few seconds of silence, followed by a ragged volley of rifle fire. We then opened fire.

We were entirely unprovided with hand-grenades, which made direct assault extraordinarily difficult. A few seconds later we heard them calling for hand-grenades. We waited, keeping up a steady fire and crawling a little closer.

Then came the hand-grenades. They pitched half a dozen of them in quick succession among us.

One of the *Guardias* lying a little in front of me to the right, got a grenade full in the back and was blown into bloody fragments of flesh and blue cloth. I recalled that he was the man who had asked the question about the meeting of the League of Nations. We continued firing.

Daily Worker, 28 September 1936

FASCIST INFANTRY TOO RATTLED TO FOLLOW UP ATTACK BY GERMAN BOMBING PLANES

For a matter of ten minutes or fifteen, the rifles cracked and the bullets zipped in the darkness, and the hand-grenades, tossed among us from the enemy position up the slope exploded loudly at irregular intervals.

Then they started getting the machine-guns into a new position commanding the slope we lay on. Machine-gun fire down that slope could, coolly and properly directed, wipe out in a couple of minutes anyone who dared to raise enough of his body above a protecting boulder to be able to see or to fire back.

A moment later the isolated whine of the rifle bullets merged into a whistling concert as the machine-gun bullets tore over us, and there was a continual loud smacking sound as the better-aimed bullets hit the rocks behind which we lay.

Fortunately the enemy was already badly rattled and the machine-gun fire was mostly over our heads.

It was agreed we should continue firing as long as possible in order to throw as big a scare into the enemy as might be, and thus frighten them out of supporting with their infantry their air attack in the morning.

Then bending double among the boulders, with a perfect hysteria of machine-gun fire going on behind, we made for a point a couple of hundred yards to the rear where the hill dipped rather sharply and gave us a sort of cover from direct fire.

At this point the belt holding my trousers broke.

It is at any time a disconcerting experience to have your pants fall suddenly about your knees. To have it happen when you are running downhill with machine-gun bullets smacking on to the boulders all round you, and people tossing hand-grenades after you to speed your departure, produces a situation which it is no exaggeration to describe as acutely embarrassing.

By the time I had squatted among the rocks and adjusted the damage as far as possible, I discovered that I was alone, the others having supposed I had fallen dead.

I reached the comparative safety of the dip in the hillside.

Lying flat behind a large stone, and cursing quietly and continuously, were five Assault Guards. They had just two rounds of ammunition per man, and no hand grenades.

We huddled close together – the Assault Guards had capacious warm cloaks – and lay flat enough to be safe from the machine-gun bullets which every couple of minutes or so suddenly shot over our heads.

'If we had hand-grenades ...' began one of the Guards for about the fifteenth time.

'If', said everyone else.

The first man, a middle-aged fellow with a fine black beard and lined thoughtful face, pursued the subject, pausing now and then to listen to the crash of heavy shells falling on our positions somewhere to the left, and a series of new outbursts of machine-gun fire away in the darkness below us, between us and the ravine we had crossed when we set out.

'I mean to say,' he said, 'you'd think that by this time there must have been time to get hand-grenades through from the democratic countries.'

'As for instance?' said another who was a member of the United Socialist and Communist Youth.

'Well,' said the bearded man 'as for instance England.' He looked questioningly at me.

The Youth member, who read the papers carefully delivered a brief and excellent analysis of the 'neutrality' situation, tracing the road all the way from the decisions of certain gentlemen in Transport House, London, England, to that black hillside where we lay without hand-grenades, and two rounds of ammunition per man.

'But the English people? The democrats?' persisted the man with the beard.

My teeth chattering noisily with the cold, I explained as well as I could.

'So it really depends on what they do,' said the bearded man. 'Well, I must say I hope it will be all right. I suppose they understand the situation. I hope it will be all right in the end.'

The conversation petered out, and we lay silent in the cold darkness, looking up at the Great Bear, shining clear after the passing of clouds above the enemy position up the hill.

'As for me,' said one of the Guards, 'I'll be damned if I try to go back before we've done a bit more to worry these swine.' The proposition was discussed back and forth and resulted in a decision to scatter and see if there was any possibility of doing any sniping. We were only to fire if we saw a clear target, and to reassemble in any case after a half hour or so. I had fifteen rounds of ammunition taken from one of our dead and this was distributed.

We scattered. At the end of twenty minutes cautious prowling, I had found no good sniping point, had fired two shots at a small body of men clustered near the corner of the enemy position, and was completely lost.

It must then have been shortly before midnight, and for the rest of that rather hair-raising night I wandered shivering about the mountain, with snipers from above firing repeatedly and hitting trees very uncomfortably close to me, and in front a constant rattle of firing showing that the Fascist positions were already between me and our own position.

I kept falling down, and once fell face downwards into a mountain stream. Soaked, I found the cold almost unbearable.

At dawn I was still a long way behind the Fascist positions, having accidentally taken a track to the left instead of the right. It was not until a couple of hours after sunrise that I finally crept up the bed of a tiny mountain stream and came out in our own lines, a mile or so below our own position.

I immediately went up the road again to our own outpost, where I was received with quite a celebration, everyone having supposed I had been dead for hours.

That morning the German bombers came again and again – as a result, prisoners told us later, of our night attack – the enemy infantry were too cold about the feet to follow it up.

Cold and filthy and sleepless for twenty-four and some for thirty-six hours, we gathered in the 'kitchen' among the rocks, and stood around, munching bread which you had to bang against the rocks to break, and large cubes of pork fat.

Standing a little way out among the rocks, leaning on his rifle one of the peasants from Albacete province began singing softly to himself a southern song. Everyone listened.

He reached the end of a verse and paused.

Into the pause broke the voice of a man from Toledo province, singing another song.

The man among the rocks stood up straight, waited till the verse was over, and then began to sing again, this time with flourishes and variations. Everyone applauded. He finished and everyone shouted, 'Come on Toledo, beat that.'

The Toledo man laid down his rifle to give his arms and chest full play and sang again, ending in a storm of clapping that echoed far out over the rocky hillside. 'Cap that one,' they shouted. 'Come on Albacete.'

The men sucking at the stony bread, some standing on the carpet of charred pine needles, others lolling on the rock ledges around the 'kitchen' listened keenly to each in turn, shouting in unison when either of the competitors in this sudden singing match scored a notable hit.

They sang verses of old peasant love songs, verses of songs about the land, patriotic songs, and new songs of the defence of Spain against Fascism.

For half an hour their voices rose alternatively in the cold morning air, sweet, grave and undaunted though a few yards away, bullets hit the rocks beside us, and at five minute intervals the whine and rustle of a big shell going over mingled with the singing.

'In some ways,' said the Captain, 'we Spaniards cannot be said to be a cultured people. Our music, however, is pretty good.'

The wind dropped, the clouds were gone, and in an hour the cold had turned to heat that made it painful to put your hand on the bare rock.

Daily Worker, 29 September 1936

FACING ENEMY MACHINE-GUNS, HE SHOUTED 'LONG LIVE DEMOCRACY!'

At one in the afternoon, when the sun glare on the bare rocks was actually blinding to the eyes, and our lack of sufficient water made our tongues seem to swell in our mouths, the Captain suggested it would be desirable, from the point of view of carrying out our delaying tactics to the full, to attack new enemy positions half-way up the opposite hill.

Some of those present opposed this on the ground they now had four machine guns in those positions, whereas we should be charging up a bare hillside, with sparse pines as cover, with no machine-gun and with very little ammunition.

'Hell,' said the Captain, 'I'm not asking anyone to come who doesn't want to. I want fifteen volunteers ...'

Yards in advance of us, the Captain – who had had half his left foot blown off years ago in Africa – limped nimbly among the rocks, a calm lean figure, six foot seven inches in height, pausing now and again to glance over his shoulder and shout encouragement to us.

The heat was terrific, the climb knocked the breath out of you, and the eternal bullets whined and smacked, killing two of our men almost at the outset, and wounding another.

In the last lap, three hundred yards from the machine gun emplacements, a young Madrid mechanic who had been elected

Corporal that morning for his gallantry during the night attack, suddenly gathered himself together like a man starting a hurdle race, and rushed forward, bounding from rock to rock faster than you could have thought any man's muscles would take him.

He was twenty, thirty, fifty yards ahead. We saw blood spurt suddenly from his elbow and stream down his left hand.

Once he put his right hand quickly to his head, and held it for a second where a bullet had zipped along his skull.

He got within sixty yards of those machine guns. There, standing among the rocks he raised a terrific voice and shouted: 'Long Live the Republic. Long Live Democracy. Down with Fascism. Down with War. Up the People. Hurrah for Freedom and Spain.'

Then he dropped among the rocks and began firing.

By the time we reached him, he was bleeding freely from four wounds. He grinned at us. 'By God,' he said, 'That frightened the bastards.'

From this position we continued firing for a matter of fifteen minutes. They must have been very badly rattled. The first comforting evidence of it we had was the fact that whereas according to all the laws of commonsense we ought to have been shot off the bare face of the earth, most of their machine-gun shooting still went high.

The people who had remained at our position on the hill behind told us bullets had been whistling through the trees there all the time, meaning very bad shooting indeed.

When we did retreat, carrying wounded with us – we had to shoot one man who was too badly wounded to have a chance of living all the way down the hill, and we knew what the Fascists would do to him if they caught him still alive – we diverged from the line we had taken on the way up, and moved over to the left where there was better cover, in the shape of a ravine running slantwise down the hill.

Halfway down we came upon a position which at the moment of our advance the Fascists had held as an advance post in front of and to the right of the machine-gun emplacement.

They had been so scared at the sight of fifteen exhausted and poorly-armed men advancing up that hillside that they had fled in panic.

They left behind them cloaks (which we badly needed), a quantity of silk shirts belonging to their commander, a couple of bottles of alcohol, and twelve brand new German automatic rifles, fresh from Essen, together with ammunition.

We returned laden with these useful objects to our own positions, having lost three dead and five more or less seriously wounded in this grim game which the ban on arms to the democrats and the permission of arms to the rebels compels the democrats to play: taking fantastic risks in hopeless but still necessary effort to even out the difference between a German-manned Junkers plane with bombs and machine-guns, and a peasant lad with eight days' training, a rifle and a few rounds of ammunition.

Morning and noon and night we played that game on the sierras. A game which is played with the lives and the young bodies of the patriots of Spain. In the bomb-scarred shell-scarred, bullet-scarred, headquarters at Guadarrama, grimy bearded men, sleepless commanders of the People's Army stood gravely about me as I prepared to leave for England.

They wanted to send a message. News of 'bombers coming over' interrupted that. 'Well,' said one of them, treasurer of the printers' union, west Madrid section, 'perhaps it doesn't matter. Perhaps you will be able to make them understand.'

'The people understand,' I said.

'Well,' he came back at me, 'the Labour Party?'

'It's not the people in the Labour Party,' I said. 'But of course there are certain leaders who ...'

'Of course,' he said.

Three days later I stood in Transport House, London, and asked for an appointment with Mr Middleton. I explained I was just from the battlefront in Spain and could possibly supply some useful information.

'Mr Middleton', said the neatly turned out gentleman-secretary, 'is very, very busy.'

'Of course,' I said. 'When will he be free?'

'I'm afraid,' said the secretary, adjusting his handkerchief in the breast pocket of his nice suit, 'I couldn't tell you that.'

'You mean to say you can't tell when he'll be free? This is rather an urgent matter, you know.'

'Well, you just leave your name and address, and then perhaps, you see, Mr Middleton can ring you.'

'When? Today? Tomorrow?'

'Oh, I'm afraid I couldn't tell you that.'

For a moment I was rather near losing my temper.

'Listen,' I said. 'You do understand, or don't you, that there is a war going on? That people are being killed while we stand here?'

'Oh, yes,' said the secretary, brightly. 'We quite understand that.'

'And you can't even fix an appointment?'

'No, I'm afraid not.'

In the meantime Mr Middleton has still not telephoned. Toledo has fallen. The casualty lists on the front line of democracy lengthen. How long?

Daily Worker, 30 September 1936

VERDUN OR A NEW COMMUNE?

MADRID, Tuesday.

The capital is in a very difficult position in organising its defence because the Fascists can literally shoot Republican soldiers with machine-guns mounted on low-flying, swooping German planes. The Fascist High Command has sent against Toledo and Madrid all their accumulated forces and arms received from abroad.

At the beginning the government air force was poor, but its relative position has worsened as a result of the so-called 'neutrality', by means of which the Fascists have been able to secure the very latest planes and other equipment.

The Fascists have a well-equipped cavalry, while the Republicans are only now forming theirs. Their superiority in forces, plus their vital necessity to consolidate themselves in the centre of the country before winter sets in, increases their determination.

Madrid will have to withstand a Fascist attack which will have every possible technical advantage.

This great city with a population of a million is nevertheless taking every possible step to drive the Fascists back. Activities for strengthening the defences on the outskirts of the city are taking place day and night.

On Sunday a number of short and stormy meetings were held,

which were attended by many thousands of people. Under rank-and-file initiative new forms of organisation are constantly being thrown up for the defence of districts, streets and separate houses. But what is known of the resources of the Fascists make us expect the worst. The Fascists will stop at nothing in their attempt to seize the city.

To be frank, the people of Madrid need not only bread, milk and water, but also gas-masks.

In the attack on Madrid the Fascist generals, with their German and Italian friends, will try to combine the experiences of Abyssinian and Shanghai bombardments with the military-chemical technique of German Fascism and the fanatical traditions of the Inquisition.

It is difficult to tell at this stage how the struggle will end; whether Madrid will go down to history as the Spanish Verdun, or will it have to share the fate of the Paris Commune.

One can be sure that Madrid will fight to the death, but world public opinion in all countries must make itself heard by raising its voice against the new and monstrous crime of mass slaughter which the Fascist war instigators are preparing.

Chapter Two

THE STRUGGLE FOR MADRID

In a later part of Reporter in Spain, *Cockburn describes the Fascist air attacks on Madrid, the reaction of the people and the Republican government, and shows how the military balance was shifting against the Republic following the involvement of the Axis powers. The newspaper reports which follow show Cockburn's return to London for a speaking tour, then his subsequent return to Spain after writing* Reporter in Spain *and his coverage of the great battles in defence of the capital in which the International Brigades played a leading part.*

XV

A Junker plane came over in the early morning and dropped leaflets from a great height up in the clear sky. 'Franco threatened bombardment.' Jose Bergamín, Catholic writer and member of the Cultural Commission of the People's Front, was reading one in the offices of the Commission.

'It is a pity', he said, 'that you are always so busy. Perhaps you don't realise that today may be your last chance for a long time to see some of the finest pictures in the world.'

The Cultural Commission, consisting of the leading artists, critics and writers of Spain, had done a great work in those weeks, enriching the art galleries and museums with treasures which sometimes were found mouldering in dark places of churches, sometimes hidden from the people's view in the locked rooms of private houses, sometimes – as though a picture were no more than a mortgage bond or a share certificate – locked in the strong rooms of the Bank of Spain, deposited there as guarantee for the debts of some grandee.

The picture galleries and the museums bloomed afresh. The list of famous and beautiful pictures discovered by the Commission and taken to the Prado for public exhibition read as though some whole new and splendid gallery had been discovered. 'Today I am afraid', said Bergamín, 'that we shall have to start hiding them all in the dark again. These brutes will bomb anything, even the Prado. We shall have to see whether the cellars can be made bomb-proof.'

Before I met him in Madrid during the civil war, I had only seen Bergamín once, at a party of writers and artists held on a roof in Hampstead earlier in the summer. Everyone was talking of solidarity, and Bergamín, in his aloof slightly bewildered way, bowed and smiled pleasantly when people spoke of the victory of democracy in Spain.

He put in a number of telephone calls in preparation for moving the Prado pictures to the cellars and we talked for a while as he waited for them to come through. He asked me for the second time to explain to him exactly the situation regarding the possibilities of unification in the British labour movement.

'You see,' he said, 'it appears to me that this is going to be an absolutely decisive question for the future of everything I believe in and love.'

We spoke of the urgency of unity, its possibilities.

In the night the bombers came.

Sirens mounted on motor-cars screamed horribly through the streets. That was before there were any bomb-proof shelters, and people dashed to the Metro stations. Fascist gunmen, held in readiness for just that, and concealed by the darkness of the threatened city, fired at random in the streets full of startled women carrying babies and leading small children to the underground.

In some places they created a panic, in others they were shot down by militia. In most, they failed to stampede people, but themselves made good their escape in the darkness. There was fairly prolonged firing in Cuatro Caminos.

Militia men ran along the corridors of the hotels, hammering on the doors, telling people to come downstairs. This was mainly a precaution against people who might keep the lights on in their rooms.

We turned out the lights, and raised the blind. You could see right across by daylight to the line of the Sierra Guadarrama. We peered out in the darkness listening for the approach of the German planes.

On the top of the Capitol building opposite, the searchlights played in all directions.

Out at one of the aerodromes there was tense waiting, as a score of pilots received orders from a 'higher officer' not to move from their barrack on the field. They knew that in the barrack next door had been carefully stored – by somebody's orders – enough high explosive to blow up the whole place.

All through the half-hour of warning before the bomber came over, the ground flares on the aerodrome, showing exactly the position of the field and the barracks and the munition dump were kept burning, by order.

When the first bomb fell there, it fell within a few yards of the munition dump, on a narrow roadway exactly midway between the barracks where the aviators were and the dump.

In the morning a certain higher officer was executed for that. Notices appeared in the Fascist press denouncing the 'blood lust' of the government forces.

In the lounge of the Hotel Florida people stumbled cautiously about among the club chairs and divans.

There was some dispute as to whether we should stay there in the lounge from which it was possible to see and hear a good deal or go to the cellar below, which was safer, but otherwise unsatisfactory.

'There's a little blonde gone down there that isn't at all bad,' said one of the Americans.

'There are probably some little blondes here if you could see them in the dark.' The speaker lit a match for a cigarette, and a voice like a pistol shot from the street ordered us to be careful with the lights.

A French woman said, 'If So-and-so goes to the cellar, I think that will be an indication that the raid is intended to be serious.' So-and-so was an American journalist, agent of a notorious financial magnate and a personal friend of Herr Hitler.

He spent much of his time in the German Embassy. He had already made himself notorious years before in Chapei where he used to be seen running like a dog after titbits, round the tables of the Fascist Japanese officers in charge of the attack on that city.

We saw him come into the lounge and make his way cautiously towards the cellar.

'Why don't you go to the German Embassy and be really safe?' someone asked him. 'The German Embassy', he said, 'has left by plane for Alicante.'

'In that case the cellar is certainly the place.'

We tried it and came up again.

Being bombed in a city seems somehow more unpleasant – more unnatural as it were – than being bombed at the front. I said so.

A Frenchman laughed. 'You call it natural to be bombed anywhere? I call it highly unnatural. Personally I am a good honest bourgeois, and I feel very much inclined to protest to somebody.'

'If your two governments go on the way they're going now,' said a young Pole, 'very soon nobody will think it in the least unnatural to be bombed at any time and in any place. It will have become a habit. Just as certain insects after a very short span of life have the habit of being suddenly set upon and done to death by other insects.'

'Listen,' said the Frenchman. 'A Pole is telling our governments how to behave to Monsieur Hitler. It will I think now be in order for myself and my English friend here to make a few well-chosen observations on the policy of Colonel Beck, his relations with Monsieur Hitler, his sell-out – if you will permit me to use so strong a term – of Poland to the Nazis.'

The Pole had wandered off and was trying to see out of the window.

'D'you hear anything coming?'

'I hear the sirens in the distance, and the lifts going up and down, bringing people from the top floors.'

'When they start to use gas we shall have first to rush to the cellar and remain there until the exact moment when the bomb explodes, then taking the lift quickly to the roof again in order to avoid the poisonous fumes.'

'And then a bomb will fall on the power station and the lift will stop working and you will get some exercise after all.'

'Listen. Don't you hear anything coming.'

'I hear people calling to one another in the streets. Apparently someone has got lost in the dark.'

'Personally I should like a nice glass of beer.'

'There isn't any.'

'What I want is coffee.'

'There isn't any.'

'Go down and tell that bloody Fascist in the cellar that we've just heard they're using gas and its too late for him to come up now.'

'Why don't somebody shoot that bastard anyway?'

'Because of the international com-pli-ca-tions.'
'Now I hear something coming. I can hear the planes.'
They came over.
'Deutschland Deutschland über alles.'
A bomb screamed down through the night air. There was a crash, turning immediately into a sudden, painful screaming of women a long way off.

XVI

In the nice garden of the British Embassy, bored militia guards played cards. On the door was a notice saying that people who, at the most urgent advice of the Embassy, cleared out of Madrid and went to England, need not be afraid that they would there find themselves destitute, for jobs would be provided for all.

Apparently there had been those among the British colony who were more afraid of economic conditions in their native land than of the enemy bombs.

I thought of that epitaph on
'The mother of children seven.
Four on earth and three in heaven.
Three in heaven thought they'd rather
Die with mother than live with father.'

For weeks the British Embassy and the Consulates had been frantically urging people to get out. They failed to produce as big a scare as they might have in the various British colonies, but they certainly tried.

There was a curious episode in Barcelona, where the acting Consul, apparently acting on brief instructions from London, sent out alarming notices urging everyone to get out, and when questioned about it, said it was because he had information indicating the anarchists were about to run amok almost any day. (This was at the end of July.)

People treated this with a certain amount of scepticism. Then the Consul, who had been away in London, suddenly arrived from there, and within a few hours declared he had information which made it absolutely imperative for everyone to go while the going was good.

What everyone wanted to know was just how and why this

gentleman arriving from London, and after consultation with the
Foreign Office, had acquired this information, which obviously
could not refer to the anarchists, since that was information he
would have much better got on the spot.

One Englishman – a staunch Conservative – even then voiced
to me his suspicion that the Foreign Office knew a great deal
more about the interventionist plans than anyone out there in
Spain supposed.

At the time when the first Junker bomber and machine-gunner
was captured at Azuaga, I rang up the British Consul, who was
then acting as Chargé d'Affaires, and asked him whether he had
been out to ascertain the exact military character of the plane.

I had myself sat in the machine-gun turrets and worked the
bomb-release levers at the very moment when the German
Embassy was demanding that the whole diplomatic corps leave
for Alicante, as a protest against the seizure of a 'civil' plane.

The Consul said he had no time to go and see it.

I asked whether the Foreign Office was in possession of the
full facts. 'Certainly,' he said.

'And is the Foreign Office proposing to take any action?'

'Oh, no, I don't think so.'

Inside the Embassy a number of old women crawled
importantly about the place, and a couple of crooks who wanted
to wangle British passports – or at least, arm-bands, demanded
to see the Chargé d'Affaires.

I said to the diplomat whom I had come to interview, 'When
my Spanish friends ask me what on earth the British government
is really up to, and why it is prepared to give away control of the
central Atlantic to the Germans by letting them control the
submarine bases of Spain, I don't know what to say. Can you
give me any reasonable explanation?'

That was not quite true. I believed I knew the explanation. I
think all the same I somehow hoped he would produce one less
unpleasant to think about.

'Well, of course,' he said breezily, 'we shall maintain an
attitude of reserve. We shall certainly have to see what sort of
arrangement we can make with General Franco. Naturally we
shall hope to make some satisfactory arrangement.'

'You are betting on that?'

I asked him about intervention.

He said: 'But what a terrible situation it would have been if we
and the French and the Germans and Italians had all been

pouring arms into Spain. Anything might have happened.'

'Nobody asks you to have all those countries pouring arms into Spain. All you are asked to do is to preserve international law instead of deliberately breaking it. Let in the arms to the friendly government, ban arms to the rebels. That is international law. Why is it not applied?'

He changed the subject.

When I left he pumped my hand warmly up and down, beaming. 'I'm so glad we had a nice talk. And you can certainly tell your Spanish friends that I have a perfectly clear conscience. You can assure them that so far as I am concerned, I'm strictly and absolutely neutral.'

Daily Worker, 29 September 1936

'HOUSE FULL' AT GREAT LONDON MEETING TO HEAR PITCAIRN

Shower of Pound Notes

(From Our Own Correspondent)

On Wednesday Frank Pitcairn arrived back in London from Spain.

On Thursday it was arranged that the *Daily Worker* should hold a meeting, so that its readers should have an opportunity of seeing and hearing the man who had taken part in the heroic struggle of the Spanish people, not merely as a newspaper correspondent reporting events, but as a militiaman, training and fighting side by side with his comrades.

On Sunday the meeting took place. Two days' notice only, yet long enough to pack Shoreditch Town Hall to the doors.

Not only every seat in the body of the hall and the gallery filled, but people standing massed all round against the walls.

A great meeting. A success from the word go. A meeting which gave people exactly what they wanted, a first-hand picture of events in Spain linked with a close-up of events at home which are playing such a big part in the working out of the Spanish situation.

Pitcairn is not a professional orator. He is happier with a pen in his hand than a microphone at his lips.

In that, indeed, lay much of the power and strength of his address. Here was drama undramatised, facts so poignant in themselves that a wrapping of fine phrases, high-falutin rhetoric would have been superfluous.

Listening to the quiet voice telling of the struggles, the dauntless courage, the invincible determination of a people fighting against odds – bewildered as to why the odds should be so heavy when there existed the 'democratic' country of Britain to reduce them at any moment – one travelled with the speaker through each of his experiences, saw with his eyes the picture he was unfolding.

Thousands of people listened in deep silence while Pitcairn spoke. When he finished, a wave of applause broke in the hall, died away and was again renewed.

Silence again when R. Palme Dutt spoke. Now we were given a biting criticism of home events, a merciless exposure of the 'neutrality' policy of the National Government and the hypocritical attitude of Labour Party and trade union leaders.

Pitcairn had moved us to sympathy and understanding. Palme Dutt roused us to anger and keen determination.

John Langdon-Davies, special correspondent of the *News Chronicle*, who was given an enthusiastic reception, filled out the picture by recounting his experience as a 'reporter who had to prove to the Spanish people that he was a human being – that is, an anti-fascist,' and by showing us the unity of the workers as it is actually being practised in Spain.

A great meeting. No wonder that when called upon by Aitken Ferguson, the chairman, to show practical support, the audience responded as one man.

Pound notes, ten-shilling notes came fluttering down from the gallery, were handed in from every part of the hall. A cheque for £15 found its way to the platform, Half-crowns, shillings came next; lastly, more than £4 in coppers.

Altogether in less than a quarter of an hour Ferguson was able to announce that £104 had been collected.

Daily Worker, 28 October 1936

SPAIN CALLS FOR WEAPONS

Every Hour Counts: Nazi Planes Over Madrid

MADRID, Tuesday.

Flying very high in the brilliant blue sky, Junker aeroplanes again visited Madrid this morning.

Crowds thronged the main streets, shading the eyes against the morning sun as they tried to get a good look at the foreign raiders.

Loudspeakers in the cafés playing 'The Girl With the Dreamy Eyes', mingled with the howl of warning sirens, the anti-aircraft guns and the shouts of newsboys selling newspapers telling of the decision of the Second International in Paris, which appeared prominently but without comment.

Late news from the front yesterday and early this morning showed that the government militia successfully resisted violent enemy pressure at a number of points.

In the present highly critical days, every hour of resistance and every delay in the enemy advance is of premier importance. I propose to show in this message that the Fascist proposition is not so strong as might be thought. Arms for the government can make that position critical.

The present week is serious, not only for Madrid, but also for the rebel generals, and for Europe. It is critical for democracy.

It will be recalled that after the fall of Toledo, General Franco announced that he would be in Madrid by 12 October. General Mola – boasting that he had a ' fifth column' of Fascist spies and saboteurs operating in Madrid itself – claimed he would take coffee in Madrid that afternoon. (Government supporters solemnly laid a little table that day in the Puerta del Sol with a notice saying that it was reserved for General Mola.)

About the same time the reactionary British press started its notorious campaign on behalf of the 'fifth column', and the British government began to compose notes to Madrid with an apparently identical objective.

Actually the big push was delayed until after the arrival on the front of the tanks and other war materials imported to Cadiz in defiance of the so-called neutrality agreement on 15 October.

It would appear it was the intention of Fascist generals not to seize Madrid but to take it with a series of swift thrusts on a fairly narrow front, stretching from Illescas on the Toledo road, to Navalcarnero, on the main western highway.

There was pressure at other points as well, but the attacks between Escorial and between Sigüenza and Guadalajara appeared to be designed chiefly to prevent the government moving troops from those points to the scene of the main threat.

Illescas and Navalcarnero both fell. Following counter-attacks by the government troops, there began at the end of last week to be signs that the rebel attack was being extended towards the Madrid-Aranjuez road, instead of being pushed directly inwards from Navalcarnero and Illescas.

Daily Worker, 30 October 1936

BIG MADRID COUNTER-ATTACK OPENS

But Spain Still Needs British Labour's Help

MADRID, Thursday.

The great counter-attack has begun. The decisive battle is getting under way. Late last night government troops re-took Algodor, on the Arraquas and Toledo railway. Early this morning the enemy had to evacuate Pinto. The People's Army this morning took Humanes, just west of Palao. Almost at the same moment they took Sesena between Illescas and Arraquas.

As I write there are unconfirmed reports that the enemy is evacuating Navalcarnero.

In a series of devastating air-raids, loyal airmen have destroyed large numbers of enemy aeroplanes and aviation material at Tablada aerodrome, where aeroplanes had just been delivered from Germany. They described this morning the havoc and destruction as the huge Junker planes burst into flame.

Politico this morning placed at the head of its page the

following cryptic but significant statement: 'When there were no other birds about, the sparrows put on the air of eagles. But when the real eagles came, the sparrows were chased ignominiously to their nests.'

Roars of cheering rolled round the Madrid front when, for the first time for nearly a month loyal planes appeared over the lines.* Soldiers threw their caps into the air and danced, villagers just behind the lines hugged and kissed one another in the streets. Two loyal planes flew over the capital this morning, a grand sight for people used to seeing nothing but Junkers and Capronis.

Tanks were seen on their way to the front. This follows Caballero's special order for the people of Madrid and the soldiers of the Republic declaring that the government has now at its disposal all the means necessary to its triumph, and closing with the order 'to attack for the final liberation of Madrid as the stronghold of the struggle against Fascism'.

That the enemy will make a new desperate attack to batter its way into Madrid before the counter-attack can take full effect is a virtual certainty. The next forty-eight hours are likely to be crucial.

In every Madrid office and factory are posted notices making arms drill and military instruction compulsory. Scores of thousands are ready to leave workshops and desks at a moment's notice if the alarm call comes. Special brigades are ready at strategic points. Work on the trenches outside the city is still in progress.

The enemy is reported to be preparing a mass tank attack on the Illescas road.

In a leading article this morning *Politico* writes: 'The wished-for twenty-four hours more has gone by. Yesterday we were patient: today we are impatient. It is not that we imagine that one day is anything to clear up the whole situation, but we do believe that within a very few days the nightmare of the enemy at the gates of Madrid will remain nothing but a memory of the most difficult days we have gone through since the beginning of the war.'

That, I think myself, is probably an excess of optimism. But it is an expression of the great wave of confidence that has swept

---

* Cockburn is referring here to Soviet aircraft; during the war, *Daily Worker* coverage was generally not explicit about Soviet aid to the Republic.

over Madrid and is at least partially justified by the fact that at long last – indeed at the eleventh hour – the counter-attack has begun.

The following proclamation was issued today by Largo Caballero, Prime Minister and Minister of War:

The Fascist band, in their long march on Madrid, have wasted their energy and drained their strength. The hour has come to deal them their death blow.

'While the traitors were losing their fighting effectiveness our forces have gained alike in cohesion and in numbers. At this moment we already have in our possession formidable mechanised armament.

'We have tanks and powerful aeroplanes. Tanks and aeroplanes are a most important weapon to beat down the enemy, but these weapons in themselves, comrades, are not enough for effective counter-attack.

'It is necessary as well that you should put into service your revolutionary will to battle. The destructive fire of the tanks and the aeroplanes must be completed by the drive forward of the infantry. It is the duty of the infantry to destroy utterly whatever remains of the Fascist forces, and to seize their arms.

'Listen, comrades! Tomorrow, 29 October, at daybreak, our artillery and our armoured trains will open fire on the enemy.

'Immediately will appear our aeroplanes, hurling their bombs upon the enemy, and throwing the enemy machine-gun fire into disorder.

'At the moment of the air attack our tanks will advance against the most vulnerable enemy positions, throwing panic in their ranks.

'This will be the moment for all our troops, so soon as they receive the orders of their commanders, to hurl themselves impetuously against the enemy, to destroy them utterly.

'The traitors to their country and those who, by deception, lies and cohesions, have followed them down the road to defeat, are going to feel at last the punishment of the people.

'Your wives, sisters and daughters, who were marked down as their victims, will be saved by your advance.

'Now that we have tanks and aeroplanes, forward comrades, forward heroic sons of the working people!'

(Signed) LARGO CABALLERO.

Daily Worker, 2 November 1936

WOMEN AND CHILDREN BLOWN TO PIECES

'Let Us Avenge Our Dead', Calls La Pasionaria

MADRID, Sunday.

For the seventh time in twenty-four hours enemy planes are flying over the open city of Madrid as I write.

Late last night thirteen bombs were dropped in the city. Earlier, a big Italian Caproni came down somewhat lower than usual over the east centre of the city, behind the central post office.

Without being low enough to aim at anything in particular, the raiders opened fire with machine-guns on streets where children were playing and women standing in milk queues.

The number of the dead in Friday's massacre has now risen to between 140 and 160. The reason for the doubt in the figures is simple and ghastly.

It is that in many cases groups of people – particularly women standing close together in queues, sometimes with babies in their arms – were torn so violently to pieces by the bombs that it was impossible to be sure how many bodies were represented by the horrible, mangled and scattered remains of flesh and bones.

One place which I saw where a bomb fell near a milk shop there were bits of flesh and brains plastered against walls many yards from the actual scene of the explosion.

Investigations made on the scene of a number of the explosions show that the bombs used are of a type which are designed not for the destruction of buildings – far less of any military objective – but for killing the maximum number of people.

The cap of the bomb is small and the excavation it makes by the impact with, for instance, the pavement, is only a couple of inches deep and a few feet across. On the other hand, the lateral explosion force is tremendous. This is quite enough to tear apart a human body many yards away.

At the same time the bombs are apparently filled with bullets, on the model of the famous French 75 mm. shells.

In every case which I examined walls near the place of explosion were scarred with bullet holes, as though from a machine-gun.

Such bombs are designed principally for use against troops moving across open country, where the objective of the bomber is not the battering down of heavy defenses, but the mowing down of men.

These are the types being used by the Fascists on the streets of Madrid. One was thrown into a children's school, where those among the little boys and girls who were not literally torn to rags were perforated and chopped by the bullets.

In forty-eight hours crowded wards of the Madrid hospitals have resounded unceasingly with terrible screams of children who do not even know why they are dying, who perhaps have never heard of General Franco and his ambitions, of Hitler and Mussolini, whose airmen threw the bombs, still less of Mr Eden and Lord Plymouth, who have worked so hard to prevent the sending of arms which would have saved those children's lives. (These bombs fell within a few hours of the British delegate to the Non-Intervention Committee solemnly recording his vote on behalf of the assertion that German and Italian planes are not here.)

Within a few hours of the first outrage, recruiting officers were besieged with volunteers demanding to be sent to the front to assist in the defeating of the Fascist forces responsible.

Pedro Rico, Mayor of Madrid, speaking to the *Daily Worker* in his room at County Hall in the middle of one of yesterday's air raids, said: 'The people of Madrid are curious people. They are capable of extraordinary gaiety and casualness; they are capable, too, of very great anger, as the anger which compels them to capture, bare-handed against machine-guns, the Montaña Barracks in the first day of the revolt. They are angry now.'

La Pasionaria, who was again in the front line yesterday, rallying the militia in face of a fierce enemy drive around the Illescas road, has written the following statement on the subject of the air attack:

'Mourning and grief today fill the hearts of the people of Madrid. The enemy is desperate in face of the courage of our airmen. Our airmen, following the most humane rules for warfare, do not go looking for open and undefended figures, nor hospitals nor schools, as the enemy does. Our airmen seek out the vital points of the enemy, his aerodromes and munition factories and points of military concentration.

'Women and children have been annihilated by the enemy bullets. How many? Many. It is not the number which is important, it is the fact.

'Among the victims was a child two months old. He fell in the same instant as the mother who gave him his life. Clasped in his mother's arms, outstretched in a final expression of defence and agony, the stones of the street were his deathbed.

'The heroic achievements of the enemy! Women and children slain by these birds of prey, murdered by international Fascism.

'Will there be a protest against these murderers from those countries who showed themselves to be sensitive about the imprisonment of those who have been accomplices in how many crimes?

'England, France, will they feel their humanitarian sentiments wounded? Women and children have fallen. Their blood is a red flag of battle, their lives a trumpet call to struggle and to vengeance.

'Murderers are at the gates of Madrid. Let us go out to destroy them and to avenge our dead. Make war like men. Never forget that our acts are ruled and directed by justice.'

Daily Worker, 5 November 1936

ENEMY AT GATES OF MADRID

Women Fortify The Streets

MADRID, Wednesday.
Clouds of smoke, huge tongues of flame and the clash and thud of incessant falling of aerial bombs. Today crossed the line just beyond Getafe and Leganés, where government troops faced a drive which has brought the enemy forces almost literally to the gates of Madrid.

Today, for the first time, the government aviation went into play on the front itself, following a new series of successful bombing raids on a string of enemy aerodromes far beyond the lines.

Beyond Getafe the government forces this afternoon, after a sensational air battle, brought down a three-engined Junker bomber. On the heights of the Madrid side of Mostoles, a terrific bombardment is in progress.

Further to the left on the Hill of the Angels, enemy artillery and bombers hurled guns and explosives into the place known as the Sacred Heart of Jesus, geographical centre of the Iberian peninsula.

Beyond the line of Getafe at Carabanchel Alto, a suburb of Madrid, the population was today being evacuated. Women and children are hard at work on fortifications.

An enemy aeroplane flew at a thousand feet down the line of Madrid's Piccadilly, the pedestrians could clearly see the machine-gunner firing into the street below.

Daily Worker, 11 November 1936

SPECIAL MESSAGE FROM PITCAIRN

MADRID, Tuesday.

There is a battle in progress such as the world has not seen for nineteen years.

In one sense it is even a greater battle than the one that saved Petrograd from the Whites. For this battle is being fought in the air as well as on land.

Above the front line, over the suburbs of Madrid, are flying fighting machines which can drop upon their enemies at a speed of 300 miles an hour.

All morning there has been a series of terrific, aerial battles above the lines. Yesterday the enemy bombers were able to fly fairly low over the city, almost every hour bombing various quarters repeatedly.

This morning, from a point on the edge of the town, I watched three Junkers approach on a bombing raid and suddenly turn and fly for their lives before a cloud of government chaser planes roaring on at them from the east.

There has been no serious raid over the city this morning, so far.

It is, of course, certain that the enemy planes will still be able to slip through and bomb the city, but for the time being the command of the air is at least equally divided.

Of the last twenty-four hours I have spent some in a front line position, where the bullets hummed like hornets in summer, some in the cellar of a house around which the shells fell every half minute, and some in Madrid itself, watching the people preparing their defence.

Last night the Fascists launched a violent attack from the west, intending to drive through the park known as the Casa de Campo, which lies all along the western edge of the town.

At the end of hours of the most terrific machine-gun and rifle battle I have ever seen, they were driven back, with losses which are probably the largest they have suffered in this war to date.

This morning we walked through positions they had held and saw the piles of their dead – little piles of five and four and three, harmless at last, withered by the machine-gun fire of the defenders of Madrid.

For the first time in the history of this continent there were in action yesterday men from every country in western and central Europe, Germans, French, Italians and Poles, marching together for the same cause.

From the four corners of Europe, men had come to do their bit to save Europe.

They are not here for money, nor are they here to 'win the war on their own'. They are here because they want to fight Fascism at the point where Fascism is launching its big attack.

There are Socialists, Communists and democrats. There are working men, and professional men and shopkeepers. There are doctors and lawyers who have given up their practices and their living simply because they know enough about the science of modern fighting to be of assistance to the new People's Army of Spain which is in process of formation.

There are men of all classes and all nationalities of western and central Europe, Germans, Italians, French, Poles, Czechs, Yugoslavs, Bulgarians, Belgians and Dutchmen. There are even a handful of Russian *emigrés*, who long ago fought against the Soviet Union and today are fighting for the people's cause in the hope that they can thus redeem the mistake they once made.

All these men, who have come to Spain from their many countries to fight, have two things in common. First, they are all of them men who know what Fascism means and are determined to do everything in their power to smash it. Secondly, they are all of them men who were either in the Great War or who since then have undergone full military training in their own countries.

For both these reasons they are able to be of inestimable value in assisting the new People's Army which is composed of men who have never fought in a big war, many of whom have never done any proper military service, and many of whom are indeed at the very beginning of their political education.

Last night I saw some of them in action, together with their Spanish comrades. For hours they had been in action against the Fascist attack. They counter-attacked. The Fascists retreated on the other side of a stream which they reckoned would be absolutely impassable under machine-gun and rifle fire.

Yet the defenders of Madrid went forward. As they fired, shouting through the night, I could hear the battle cry of freedom, the slogans of democracy, shouted in nine languages.

They hurled off their heavy sheepskin coats and plunged into the stream. All around, on the water, the bullets whizzed and ricocheted. Some put their heads down and swam, others waded, bending so as to keep as much of their bodies as possible under the surface.

Into the freezing wind they emerged from the stream and charged again. The Fascists retreated. The defenders reached an advanced position, and for the whole of the rest of the night remained there firing while the wind froze the dripping clothes on their bodies.

In this fashion was beaten off one of the most desperate attempts to enter Madrid.

Up to the moment of writing there is no change on the southern front. The battle continues.

In Madrid itself every strategic crossroad has now its sandbagged barricades. It is good to see these modern barricades replacing the traditional stone barricades the workers of Spain had long believed were the proper and sufficient working-class defence, even against tanks and machine-guns.

The atmosphere grows continually more healthy. I do not mean by that that Madrid is saved, or that the Fascist attack has by any means been defeated. This is not so. The position could scarcely be graver. But I do mean that at last Madrid is, so to speak, stripped for fighting.

Daily Worker, 21 November 1936

HOW MADRID DUG IN ITS HEELS – AND STRUCK BACK!

Men Are Flocking From All Over Europe ... To Help Save Europe

The first week in November was as bad as it could be. The government counter-attack, intended to push Franco's army back down the Tagus Valley, fizzled almost before it had begun.

In some sectors it never began at all. Within forty-eight hours it had in all sectors turned with horrifying swiftness into quick, disorderly retreat towards the capital.

The attack itself – easy to say now, but still true – was premature. The material intended to be used in it was not yet ready.

The material superiority of the enemy was still enormous. The men of the People's Army had faced that superiority for a month and a half. Armed as they were, the Brigade of Guards itself could not have withstood Franco.

When Franco, swinging northward from the natural north-south front across the river valley from the sierra to the mountains of Toledo, pivoted his front on its left flank and moved to the attack on the capital, he offered opportunity for counter-attack.

If war were chess, fought with exactly equal forces and all the moves calculable, Franco would have been finished at that moment.

If the government had at that moment possessed a striking force capable of taking ordinary aggressive action in the field, that pivoting movement would have been fatal.

The government possessed no such force.

It had neither the material – the guns, tanks, aeroplanes and machine-guns – essential for the delivery of such an attack, nor, at that moment, an infantry capable of carrying it out.

I have no space here to describe the exact condition of the People's Army at that moment, nor the reasons for it.

It is enough, however, to sum it up by saying that for reasons, some of which are obvious and others less obvious, it had taken longer than two months to create an army capable of fighting a modern war out of the tens of thousands of militarily untrained workers, whose heroism had saved Spain at the end of July, but who since then had been called upon to face a very different sort of conflict against an enemy backed by the material resources of the German and Italian military machines.

Sabotage by Fascists remaining in the officer ranks of the government forces played its usual role.

In that first week of November an officer of the government forces came racing in a motor car down the Toledo highway from Torrejón to Parla and reported the enemy were already in Torrejón, the government troops in rout along the road, and artillery fire by the government batteries against Torrejón an urgent necessity.

The batteries opened fire.

They had been dropping shells into Torrejón for twenty minutes before it was discovered that the officer's story was a lie, and that the shells were dropping from behind onto government militia already facing desperate odds in front.

Soon after that the officer in question was shot, and the militia did retreat, and the enemy did get into Torrejón.

From skyscrapers in Madrid you could see, through field glasses, the Moorish cavalry coming up from the south.

On the dreadful day when they took Getafe, a telephonist was the last man to remain at his post, thus adding one more achievement to the almost incredible acts of heroism performed throughout this war by the workers of the telephone and telegraph services in Spain.

The main body of government troops left the village under appalling bomb and shell attack which killed in half a day a third of all the young children of the place.

They were blown to pieces while they played in the street. The German Fascist aviators went on throwing bombs on them as they tried to run for shelter.

That any of those wounded were saved from slow and agonising death is due to the Scottish ambulance whose members, as usual, faced daily and hourly as a matter of course risks as great, and often greater, than any front-line soldier faces.

When the last government troops moved out they tried to bring the telephonist along with them. He said he would, he must, stay to the very end to pass back the very latest information of the enemy movements.

He kept on the line. His voice came through evenly every few minutes.

He could see the enemy coming down the road. 'I can see the Moors. Now I can hear them yelling. They are yelling louder. They are in the street. Here they come …'

His voice ended and the listeners at the other end could hear quite clearly, like the voice of barbarism, close in the ear of civilisation, the high, wild cries of the African invaders imported against Europe by Franco, Mussolini and Hitler.

The government, which ought to have left several weeks before in order to carry on its civil functions without getting them tangled up in the necessary war machinery of a nearly front-line town, at last consented to quit the capital and go down to Valencia.

In all the terrific story of the Spanish civil war, and the defence of Spain and Europe against Fascism, there is to my mind nothing more uplifting or more touching to the heart and the head than the story of how the people of that great menaced capital, with the enemy at the gates, the army outclassed, the bombers overhead, the shells of the heavy guns falling in the city; attacked from without, stabbed at from within, deserted and betrayed by those foreign governments that should have been its friends, and filthily slandered in the press of all the millionaires of the world, declared by all the experts to be defeated, lost, and done for, at the eleventh hour did begin to dig in its heels and fight.

All that evening the loudspeakers shouted in the cafés, in the streets, and in a hundred thousand homes, giving no music except the grim, beautiful music of the common people going into action on behalf of the simplest rights of suffering humanity.

The bands and the choirs were silent. Instead came pouring from the loudspeakers the orders of mobilisation.

'All members of the Bakers and Allied Workers' Association will report themselves to the barracks of the militia of the Association at seven o'clock tomorrow morning without fail or exception. No excuses will be considered valid for failure to comply with this order of the association.'

'Hullo, Hullo …

'Hullo, hullo … all members of the United Youth organisation not already on the front will report themselves at seven o'clock tomorrow morning at the barracks of the militia of the said organisation. No excuses will be considered valid for failure to comply with this order of the organisation.'

'Hullo, hullo … all workers of the National Union of Teachers between the ages of 17 and 55 will report themselves at seven o'clock tomorow morning at the barracks of the militia of the above organisation. No excuses will be considered valid for failure to comply with this order of the National Union.'

'Hullo, hullo … all workers …'

The *Mundo Obrero* issued a manifesto to the women, instructing them that tomorrow they must carry their men's meals, not to the factories, as they used to do, but to the trenches of the front line.

The enemy were that close.

The Fifth Regiment printing presses were busy turning out hundreds of thousands of leaflets giving instruction in how to defend the houses and streets of the city against tank and armoured car attack.

In every house committees of defence were being formed.

Everywhere searches were being made for the arms known to have been hidden all over Madrid by members of General Mola's 'fifth column' –the organisation of traitors and terrorists maintained in the capital by the Fascist enemy, whose existence had been openly admitted by General Mola at the beginning of October.

There is no space even to begin a list of the crimes committed by the members of the fifth column.

One of their achievements gives you an idea of how the thing was intended to work. At the time of the first of the really serious air raids in Madrid, when nearly 200 people, of whom two-thirds were women, were blown to pieces by bombs, it was immediately noted with surprise that a very large proportion of the bombs thrown had actually fallen into the very middle of queues of women waiting for milk and coal to be distributed.

At first it was thought that this was simply a horrible accident. Then, as eye-witness stories of some of the explosions began to come in, and as the doctors made expert examination of the wounds caused, it was realised that there was more in it than accident.

From eye-witness stories – I talked to one myself who had seen the bombing of the milk queue on Fuencarral Street – it was established that in a certain number of cases the bombs had not been thrown from aeroplanes at all. They had been thrown from the windows, at the moment of the air raid.

One, for instance, was thrown from the upper window of a house midway between the offices of the UGT and the CNT. Another, at the very moment when an aerial bomb fell further down the street, was thrown straight into a coal queue from the roof of an opposite house.

It was quite easy for the organisers of the fifth column to keep in touch by means of secret radio transmitters and code receivers with the enemy command outside.

The bomb outrages were thus able to be timed more or less exactly, so that all the terrorists would be at their posts at the moment when the planes came over the city. The dropping of the aerial bombs was to be the signal, for the throwing of the hand bombs from the windows.

The advantage of this arrangement is obvious.

The Fascist fifth column was busy trying to spread defeatism and demoralisation among the people. Some of their principal propaganda efforts were, of course, centred on the food and fuel difficulties of the population. They were particularly hopeful of being able to spread defeatism among the women who sometimes had to stand for six and seven hours at a time in order to get milk and coal.

They calculated that if in addition to the grim discomfort of such waiting, the queues were found to be exposed to aerial bombing, there was a good chance of getting a real panic under way.

Unfortunately for them, you cannot be sure that an aerial bomb dropped from a great height will fall in any particular street – let alone in a particular queue waiting outside a particular shop in that street.

That was why the fifth column decided to make certain of giving the full political effect to the bombing.

That is why the casualties among the women in the queues

were so high.

That is why the Spanish people says what it does about the 'humanitarian', 'impartial' efforts of Mr Eden on behalf of Fascist members of the fifth column in the jails of Madrid.

From the main streets you could already hear quite clearly the machine-gun and rifle fire at the front.

Already shells began to drop within the city itself. Already you could see that Madrid was after all going to be the first of the dozen or so big European capitals to learn that 'the menace of Fascism and war' is not a phrase or a far-off threat, but a peril so near that you turn the corner of your own street and see the gaping bodies of a dozen innocent women lying among scattered milk cans and bits of Fascist bombs, turning the familiar pavement red with their gushing blood.

There were others besides the defenders of Madrid who realised that, too.

Men in Warsaw, in London, in Brussels, Belgrade, Berne, Paris, Lyons, Budapest, Bucharest, Amsterdam, Copenhagen ... all over Europe men who understood that 'the house next door is already on fire' were already on the way to put their experience of war, their enthusiasm and their understandings at the disposal of the Spanish people who themselves in the months and years before the Fascist attack had so often thrown all their energies into the cause of international solidarity on behalf of the oppressed and the prisoners of the Fascist dictatorships in Germany, Hungary and Yugoslavia.

It was no mere 'gesture of solidarity' that these men – the future members of the International Brigade – were being called upon to carry out.

The position of the armies on the Madrid fronts was such that it was obvious that the hopes of victory must to a large extent depend first on the amount of material that could be got to the front before the German and Italian war machines smashed their way through, and secondly, on the speed with which the defending force of the People's Army could be raised to the level of a modern infantry force, capable of fighting in the modern manner.

The Spaniards did not experience the Great War, and the training received in the form of compulsory military service was of the sketchiest and most antiquated description.

Whereas in every other great European country there is scarcely an able-bodied worker over the age of thirty-seven who did not have some considerable experience of the Great War, in Spain there is scarcely a worker who until the present civil war had had any experience whatever of modern methods of combat.

In any English town you will find certainly a score and probably upwards of a hundred working men who know how to handle some form of machine-gun.

You will find as many, probably more, who know how to throw hand-grenades. You will find hundreds who have received a fairly thorough training in bayonet fighting and also in, at least, the elements of infantry tactics.

In the European countries, in addition to this, there are the men who, without having been old enough to fight in the Great War, have done one or two years' compulsory military service under conditions very different from that morass of incompetence and traditionalism which was the old Spanish army.

It was thus that the anti-fascists of Europe were able to come to the help of the Spanish people, and at the same time get the chance to fight Fascism not among the smoking ruins of their own homes, but on the soil of Spain, with the good hope that victory over Fascism there may yet save London and Birmingham and Paris and Brussels and Lille from the foulness of destruction launched by the Fascists against Madrid.

When the call came these men came rushing from all the corners of Europe.

They hid themselves under railway carriages in the freezing nights of central Europe and while above their heads sleeping car passengers took a last liqueur and prepared for a night's rest before tomorrow's winter sports, these men hung on the steel rods like grim death, on their way to fight in Spain.

They clubbed together and hired special trains.

They travelled in private cars and lorries, and in the holds of liners and in cargo boats.

Behind them stood the resources of the genuinely militant anti-fascist working-class organisations of every country, and of all those tens of thousands of professional men and small business men who know that the struggle against Fascism is for them a life and death struggle.

They had excellent new rifles, plenty of machine-guns. And they knew how to use them, knowing equally how to fight and what they were fighting for, which are two inseparable things in the creation of a real fighting force by, of, and for the people.

At the very moment when things looked blackest these men were on their way into Spain.

They are still going in.

There are thousands of them now on the front, others on the way up to the lines, others finishing their training in the bases, and thousands more in every capital and industrial area of Europe, preparing to answer the urgent call to action – and action now.

Daily Worker, 25 November 1936

LOYALIST GENERALS JOIN COMMUNISTS

Started With 200, It Became A Division

From the office in Juan March's palace where Antonio Mije (pronounce it Mee-hay) sits as Councillor for War on the Madrid Defence Council today, it seems a far cry to the old offices of the *Mundo Obrero* in mid-July, where leader-writers urged the government to take more drastic defence measures against the coming Fascist attack, while other members of the staff took turns on guard with pistols behind a barricade of mattresses.

It is a long line, but a straight one.

That the most responsible post in the Defence Council should be held by the representative of the Communist Party (working man, militant, MP since February, member of the Central Committee of the Communist Party) is no accident.

People would have been very much surprised if the post had been entrusted to anyone else.

For all the way from July to November, and from the storming of the Montaña barracks to the trenches on the Manzanares, the Communist Party, with José Díaz, Pasionaria and Mije among its most prominent leaders, has been earning a reputation for common-sense thinking, organisational capacity and military drive, which today is immense and universal.

It is difficult to convey briefly and accurately the feeling for the Communist Party – so young, and until recently so small – which exists in Spain today.

It is not on the other hand, difficult to understand it.

As the situation grew tougher and tougher and more people who had previously been suspicious of, and even hostile to the Communist Party, began – sometimes rather grudgingly and sometimes 'with full acknowledgments' – to accept the fact that a great many things the Communists had said, which seemed sensational or alarmist at the time, were, as a matter of fact, true: that when the Communists talked about the 'need for unity' they really were talking about a matter of life and death, as obvious and urgent as the provision of machine-gun ammunition and sandbags: that when the Communists declared that every other political consideration must be secondary to the question of how to win the war, they meant just that: that when they called upon others to subordinate sectional aims to the need for supporting the democratic government of Spain against the Fascists they were the first to put their propositions into practice: and above all, that, as a result of their highly disciplined yet highly democratic form of organisation, they were able more easily than any other single organisation to translate intentions into action.

Of course it would be possible to put all this in a more formal way, and a full analysis of the work of the Communist Party in the united defence of Spain by all the parties of the People's Front would be a very valuable thing.

Here, since the part being played by the Communist Party in the defence of Madrid is now in the centre of the world stage, I only want to draw attention to one or two of the points which have brought the Communist Party to this immensely responsible and honourable position in the democratic alliance, where it shares with Socialists, Republicans, anarchists and Catholics, the task of holding the front line of the world's democracy against the world Fascist threat.

It is, for instance, no secret that the very first move for the creation of the People's Army of Spain came from the Communist Party. Nor did it come simply in the form of a 'suggestion' or a manifesto or a report.

It came in the form of a request for permission from the government to form a force to be known as 'The Fifth Regiment of the People's Militia'.

The government, knowing the magnitude of the task, suggested they begin by calling it a battalion. The Communists replied that a regiment was what they had set themselves to create, and a regiment they were perfectly capable of creating.

Within a few weeks, after a start with 200 men, it became necessary to consider forming the Fifth Regiment into a Division. Today it has sent to the front more than 32,000 men, of all parties and creeds, including Catholics, and the Fifth Regiment is recognised by Spanish and foreign military experts alike as the most effective of all the Spanish fighting forces at the disposal of the government.

In July the Communist Party had urged the necessity of arming the workers against the coming attack.

In September, when the conflict had very evidently taken on the full character of a modern war, the Communist Party and the Fifth Regiment took the lead in demanding that the militia, in which the traditions of the street fighting of July were still strong, should be unified and 'militarised' under a single command, as an absolutely necessary preliminary to the effective carrying on of the struggle under the new and changed conditions.

An indication – and a very important one – of the effectiveness of the Communist Party's war work is offered by the fact that today the majority of the loyal generals, not to mention the younger loyal officers, have applied for and received membership of the Communist Party.

Throughout, the Communist Party has worked in the closest co-operation with the leadership of the UGT, and it was as a result of this co-operation that the all-important step of appointing Political Commissars for work in the People's Army was adopted.

The Chief of the Council of War Commissars is Alvarez del Vayo, with Antonio Mije as a member of the Council.

Nobody will ever forget the work done by Díaz, Mije, and Pasionaria in the front line during the terrible retreats on the Aranjuez and Illescas roads, when they walked into the front lines and rallied thousands of men who, faced with an overwhelming superiority in tanks and aeroplanes, were already engaged in a withdrawal that might at any moment have turned into actual rout.

The work of Mije in the organisation of the defences of Madrid itself, of Díaz and Pasionaria and of the newspaper *Mundo*

Obrero in 'getting Madrid on its toes' to meet the enemy at the gates is an historical event as important as anything that has happened in our lifetime.

Finally, it is worth noting that, at the moment when reactionary newspaper correspondents were predicting an outbreak of terrific disorder and violence in Madrid as the enemy hammered at the suburbs, Madrid became quieter, better disciplined and more perfectly orderly than at any time in its history as a city, for the reason that the Defence Council had seen fit to entrust the maintenance of peace and public order within the capital to the United Socialist and Communist Youth.

Daily Worker, 5 December 1936

NEW HEROES SPRING TO FILL BEIMLER'S PLACE

I see by the papers that Hans Beimler was killed in Madrid on Tuesday.

Eighteen days ago we were sitting in a front line position on the Casa de Campo front outside the city, and he eased himself up to pull a map or something out of his pocket, and a bullet missed his head by millimetres.

I remarked it was a narrow shave.

He said he had seen narrower.

For instance, he was arrested by the Nazis in Munich in 1934, and after being savagely beaten at the Brown House, was taken up to the Dachau concentration camp.

What happened to him there he has told in his remarkable book, *In the Hands of Hitler's Hell Hounds*.

(By the way, I would mention the curious fact that there does not seem to be a bookseller in London that has the book in stock – although it was a best-seller in the United States and did pretty well over here. Could it be – now that Herr Von Ribbentrop and his boys are spending so much money on treasonable propaganda over here – that books like Beimler's just drop out of sight, so that even booksellers who would like to be selling them somehow lose track of where the book is to be got?)

The narrower shave happened at the end – the very end – of Beimler's period in the camp.

One night around, so far as I can recall what he told me, midnight, the Nazis came along to his cell and gave him a piece of rope.

They told him to hang himself.

They told him if he had not hanged himself by five in the morning they would be back at that time and would do the job for him.

The man in the next door cell committed suicide. (All this is described much more exactly in the book, but I am giving it as he told it me himself the other day in the Casa de Campo when there were a lot of other things already that had happened since to blur the recollection in his mind.)

After, or about the same time as the man next door gave up and hanged himself, Beimler, worn out with constant beatings, flogged repeatedly within an inch of his life, and at the same time having to work like a slave long hours all day doing the hardest kind of manual labour, began to wonder whether after all this might not be the only way out.

He told me how easy it is to figure that the 'easiest' way out is really the 'only' way out, so that what you want to do becomes, after a very short time, what you 'must' do – the only thing to do.

He very nearly did commit suicide there and then – making an end to all the horrible physical pain and agony, not to mention the mental pain and agony that went with it.

Then he pulled himself together and calculated that after all a dead man is a dead man, and utterly harmless and useless, and that he might anyway make one more effort.

The effort could, and probably would, fail, and then he would die: but he would die any way if he made no such effort.

And there was an outside chance he might succeed, and then perhaps he would live to fight new battles, and out of his own experience and his own understanding of what Fascism means and of what disunity in the face of Fascism means, he might yet strike against Fascism blows even more damaging than any he had struck in his long work as an official of the Bavarian Communist Party, before and after the Party became illegal.

He set himself with a terrific effort to think along these lines so as to overcome the fatigue and the hopelessness which threatened, after all that time in the hands of the Fascists to overcome him and nullify him.

He did so overcome it.

He began to plan how he might by a supreme effort even now, with only a matter of four and a half hours, less perhaps by now, to live at all, yet live, yet win.

And between midnight and five in the morning, with the rope there in the cell and the guards due to come at five and finish off the job, he did, as a matter of fact escape.

Nothing could have looked more hopeless than his situation at midnight, and at five he was out, and later he was over the border and writing his exposure of Fascism and what it means to the working-class.

He had been as near death as any living man has ever been, and yet by his own effort of thought and will, made possible, of course, only by a deep Marxist understanding of the importance of life and death at particular historical moments, caught all his energies together for a last thrust, and won.

Three weeks ago at a headquarters building behind the lines I saw the tall, spectacled figure of Ludwig Renn, the artillery officer and anti-war author, stepping down the pathway accompanied by another figure I did not know.

That was Beimler.

He had been on the Aragon front with the Thaelmann Centuria.

Then came the news of the formation of the International Column.

From the relative stalemate of the Aragon front, where he had already done tremendous work in helping the German anti-fascists show the Spanish anti-fascists how a modern war is fought, Beimler went to the base to join the International Column as Political Commissar.

He went up to Madrid to interview General Kléber and some other people, and in two hours had managed to get himself into the front line.

He was pulled out of there to go back to the base and do his job of political organiser there.

He told me he expected to be away at least three weeks.

Ten days later he was back again. The situation had become hotter and tougher. He refused to leave the Madrid front, saying, quite correctly, that things had developed faster than anyone had supposed and that his place as Political Commissar was there.

I think I have never seen a man who seemed so confident and happy.

He was without illusions.

He had seen the front. He had seen the casualties. He knew what the difficulties and the dangers were.

Yet, he was happy because I suppose he was entirely on the stretch, engaged in something which he knew to be a decisive action for the liberation of the world from the threat of Fascism and war which hangs over us.

He was happy because at the very moment when the news of the murder of Edgar Andre in Hamburg reached us in Madrid, he and the men of the International column were already beginning to avenge the death of Andre.

He was happy because as a genuine internationalist he had seen such sights as no internationalist has ever been privileged to see before: he was there in the Casa de Campo when Germans and Frenchmen and Englishmen and Poles and Yugoslavs, united and joined in glorious purpose as never before in European history, charged the horrid ranks of Franco's Moors and destroyed them entirely.

He was happy when I told him how the British people, despite the efforts of its open enemies in the National Government and its secret enemies in the labour movement, was slowly perhaps, but still surely, fighting its way into action on behalf of Spain, and of its own salvation.

I remember the expression on his face when he shot a deserting officer of the militia who, while his men stood firm, jumped from his post on the front line and tried to run for safety. Beimler shot him, and the men cheered and held on.

He was one of the happiest, briskest men I have ever seen and if you had told him that today he would be dead, that would have made no difference to him, except that maybe he would have fallen to thinking how much good he could do for our side and for Europe, and how much harm to the Fascists, in the little time that remained to him.

I remember how annoyed he was one night in University City, when he had arranged a little conference with some of the other political commissars and the enemy started shelling the building, and the whole conference had to be moved from an upstairs room to the cellar.

He understood, of course, that it would be silly for everyone not to go down to the cellar. At the same time he was in a frenzy of hurry to get the conference started and the decisions taken, so as everyone could get on the job as soon as possible.

I can see him now, standing with a curious doubt on his face, trying to decide whether the fifteen minutes' delay in changing the conference room was really worthwhile – and the bombs bursting all around the building and shells already skimming the roof.

It is sad for us that Hans Beimler has been killed.

It is not possible for us ever to express fully our sadness and our respect for the men who have lost their lives – Englishmen, Germans, Frenchmen and a dozen other nationalities – fighting for the peace and the progress of the world in one of the greatest movements of genuine international solidarity the world has ever seen.

It is sadder still for the Nazis, for international Fascism, for the enemies of the people everywhere, that they should have been up against a man like Hans Beimler, who, when they thought they had him for sure, with five hours to decide between forced suicide and murder, yet had the willpower, the training, the discipline, the knowledge, to break out and to insist that he should live to fight new battles against them.

You often read in the papers that someone's death has produced an 'irreplaceable loss'.

In our movement it is not so.

Nobody would have been more disgusted than Hans Beimler if you had told him that his place could not be filled. He knew and we know that his place can and must be filled.

At the very moment when Nazis thought they had killed Edgar Andre, they found that from the blood of that great leader of the forces of democracy and freedom had sprung the Battalion which smashed the attack that was to have taken Madrid.

We have often said that from the blood of our murdered comrades new men, new champions would spring.

Perhaps there were people who thought that was just a phrase we used: a way of saying things not meaning anything very concrete and real.

Today they know that when the people claims it will send new men to fill the places of every man that falls, the people means what it says.

The new champions are really there. They are there in that roaring semi-circle of shell fire, bursting bombs, gas, machine-gun bullets and mud, around the city of Madrid, the men of the International Brigade.

A month ago there was scarcely a person in Britain who had heard of the International Brigade.

For very practical reasons we have been in a position to see just how Britain has responded to the knowledge of that Brigade's existence when it got that knowledge.

Betrayed by a treacherous government, befuddled and bemused by place-seekers, sell-outs, crooks, intriguers and cowards in its own ranks, the people of England has yet shown and will not cease increasingly to show that the people of England – sending men to fight, doctors and ambulances to the battlefields, food, overcoats, and all the necessities of men at war, to the base camps – understands not only the urgency of victory, but the way to it.

Daily Worker, 14 December 1936

SPAIN NOW SINGS 'TIPPERARY'

'British Best of Battalion'

MADRID, Sunday.

In a lot of towns and villages between here and the coast this week, people have been learning a new song; it is 'Tipperary'. The British volunteers of the International Column are marching in.

In Barcelona and Valencia and other places I came through a week ago, they were asking me whether more English were coming. A few days later they were there, small groups of four and five at a time, some of them almost overwhelmed by the great cheering crowds that turned out to welcome them. They were almost too hoarse to speak on account of having spent several hours showing half the population of Valencia how to shout:

> 'One, two, three, four, five,
> We'll get Franco dead or alive.'

These are the real volunteers. Yesterday, in the candlelight of the vast rest barracks, 'somewhere behind the front', I met veterans of the British contingent. They have been here since the end of October. They are one of the machine-gun sections of the machine-gun company of the 2nd Battalion of the First International Brigade.

Here is what Alfred Brugère, young French commander of the machine-gun company, has to say about them.

'The British troops have given nothing but the most absolute satisfaction. Alike on the front and in the rest camp their calm conduct is the best of the entire battalion. They have been praised for special valour by all the commanders of the company. How happy I should be if I could have a whole company made up of such men.

'The British section of our machine-gun company is magnificently representative of the best elements of the British people, and the anti-fascists of Britain will be proud of them.

'I send my greetings to all anti-fascist comrades in Britain, and I call upon them to push forward even more vigorously the campaign to alter the government's policy towards the legitimate government of Spain.'

The men of whom the Commander was speaking are: John Cornford, John Sommerfield, Bernard Knox, Edward Burke, David Mackenzie, Joe Hinks, Thomas Batten, Joe Stephens, B. Symes, R. Sowyer, W. Berry, and one other, who does not want his name to be mentioned. If any single group of men have a claim to have played a leading part in the eleventh-hour saving of Madrid, these men have that claim.

As we lay wrapped in blankets on the stone floor of their barracks behind the front last night they told me part of their story.

It was when things were at the worst, and they were rushed from the base far back in eastern Spain into the line around the menaced city. When the lorries in which they were brought up reached the city of Vallecas they had been thirty-six hours without sleep and almost without food.

That evening they were served with machine-guns of the only type available to the defenders. Imagine their feelings when they found that it was a gun which none of them had ever seen before, and which nobody in the whole machine-gun company knew how to work.

Imagine the courage and tenacity of these men, who spent the night before the battle sitting down in flickering candle light

around new guns, practising over and over again how to take the
gun to pieces, to remount it and work it. That was how they
spent the night and by morning they knew how.

By evening the Moors, too, knew that the British had come,
and knew to their cost that they had learned how to fire a gun.

Ever since then the British group has been in the forefront on
every occasion.

Edward Burke, who a few weeks ago sat in the editorial office
of the *Daily Worker*, was found to possess an extraordinary flair
for machinery. In the first big attack of the International column
in the Casa de Campo one of the first machine-gun sections
asked that he should be lent to them.

When in the attack the French Commander of the section was
killed, although there were several men in the section who had
served for years in the Foreign Legion, they asked Burke to take
over the command. He recently returned to join the other
comrades of the English troop.

Joe Hinks is one of the heroes of a terrible fight near Humera,
when a tiny troop of British and French machine-gunners were
surrounded by the overwhelming forces of the Moors. For
one-and-a-half days they were given up for lost.

It was Joe Hinks who finally made it possible for them to get
their way out. Firing his Lewis gun from the hip, he covered
their escape.

Joe is foremost in the battle as a man who never fires a shot
unless he has something to fire at, and has been much praised
for his economy of ammunition. Yet, in a thirty-six hour battle
he had to fire from a Lewis gun and rifle no less than 1,800
rounds.

David Mackenzie, nineteen-year-old school teacher and
medical student from Edinburgh, is equally famous as a shot.

He is now a first-class Lewis gunner and recently – from a
position in the Philosophy and Letters Building in University
City – shook out an entire enemy machine-gun section with one
burst of Lewis gunfire at 750 yards' range.

I wish everyone who has supported and is supporting the
International Column could have been there in the barracks last
night to hear these men's stories from their own lips.

When I asked Cornford – who had his head bandaged from a
sabre wound – and Sommerfield to talk about the experiences,
they both kept saying, 'Well, I don't know why they keep
thinking we have done such great things. Looking back, it does

not seem as though we had ever done anything very special'.

It was at this point that the French Commandant came into the conversation. 'No,' he said, 'we have not done anything special – except to help our Spanish comrades save Madrid.'

Daily Worker, 15 December 1936

BRITISH FIGHTERS NOW POURING INTO SPAIN

'Veterans' As Trainers of 'Recruits'

MADRID, Monday.
New reinforcements for the International Anti-fascist Column are now pouring in.

The fourth all-British company has arrived, and was greeted with tremendous enthusiasm by the population of Madrid.

You have to see Madrid to understand the huge prestige, the admiration, which the International Column has acquired for itself among the Spanish people at whose disposal they have put their fighting ability. Already the British troops are famous throughout the column as a model first-class fighting force against Fascism.

Soon, it is to be hoped, we shall have our own British battalion.

It is possible that the British troops already on the front will be shortly sent down to the base camps to assist in the organisation of the new recruits into the first all-British company.

When I passed through the base camps a few days ago steps were already being taken to unify the various British troops who are at present scattered in various camps to which they were sent on arrival.

I saw Ralph Fox there, anxious to get to the front immediately, and at the same time doing a big job at the base acting as the first Political Commissar.

Tom Wintringham, with hands and overalls glistening with

machine-gun oil, was described to me as one of the best
machine-gun experts they had.

He had been going through a stiff course of machine-gun
training in order to familiarise himself perfectly with the different
types of machine-guns which are to be used by the defending
troops.

This course completed, he will be appointed as a machine-gun
officer of the new British company, or possibly brigade
machine-gun officer, in the nearest brigade of the International
Column.

As a part of the 'militarisation' of the People's Army, which
the International Column has done much to inspire, it was
announced yesterday that those troops and militia which are not
yet properly integrated in companies and battalions of the army,
should from today organise on a proper military basis.

What the 'militarisation of the army' really means is the
organisation of hundreds of troops of militia – trade union
militia, professional militia, intellectual militia, local militia,
peasants' militia, etc., which sprang into existence in the early
days of the civil war – into a force capable of conducting war
under conditions existing when the forces of the people, instead
of simply defending their cities against the attacks of Fascist
officers, have to meet the armies of international Fascism in
modern field warfare.

Meanwhile, the Fascists continue at intervals to throw shells
from modern field artillery on to the homes of the civilian
population of Madrid.

It was announced yesterday that about 60,000 people, of
whom about half are small children, have been evacuated from
the city.

But there remain, even now, families, including thousands of
children, who, as a result of the ruthless attack on civilians
carried out by Fascist bombers, are now living on the platforms
of the underground railways.

For a woman whose husband is fighting at the front or on the
barricades, it is sufficiently terrible and heartbreaking to have to
take care of a family of children on an underground railway
platform – particularly as from time to time one of the new
torpedo bombs of German make pierces the roadway and
crashes through to the underground railway.

But adding to the horror of the situation is the new factor of
piercing cold.

A biting wind that cuts through even a warm overcoat has sent the temperature tumbling in Madrid. Every morning in the streets you can see tiny groups of people – old women, little boys and girls – struggling with huge lumps of wood which they are trying to carry to their homes or places of refuge.

Some of them have stood in the freezing wind since five or six o'clock in the morning to get this wood which they are now scarcely able to lift. Harassed by air raids for weeks, pierced by cold, they still wait calmly in those early morning queues – as calmly and cheerfully as people waiting to enter a cinema.

These are the people whom Franco says he is disheartening. These are the magnificent people whom the International Column is helping to save from bloody destruction by Fascist gunmen.

80 Irishmen Joining International Column

Eighty men have left Ireland to fight in the Irish division of the International Column in Spain. Within the next few days this number will be increased to 200.

They are led by Mr Frank Ryan, Irish Republican leader. He says that this is 'a demonstration of the sympathy of the revolutionary Irish workers with the Spanish people in their fight against international Fascism'.

Daily Worker, 17 December 1936

PITCAIRN SEES MURDER DONE BY FRANCO'S GANG

MADRID, Wednesday.

Franco's forces, after their costly defeat of yesterday, this morning again attacked violently on the north-western sector of the Madrid front.

They were apparently attempting a new push towards the Madrid-Escorial road.

Parallel with their military attack, the Fascists today again adopted their murderous tactics of assault upon the morale of the civilian population.

On the way back from the front this morning I had a front seat view of these tactics in operation.

It was at the village of Majadahonda. This little village, which looks like a country village in Essex, is not on the front, and there are no troops in it. There is nobody in it except the civilian population, which lives in a couple of score of small houses on the village street, and a few farm houses by the village pond, a little way from the road.

We were standing in the main street tinkering with the car when we saw the planes, twenty Caproni bombers, flying low in very close formation.

People ran down the street telling the villagers to run into the fields. There were women running with little children in their arms, and others trying to explain to little boys and girls as they dragged them by the hand that they must run faster, faster.

We reached a sunken field track a couple of hundred yards between the road before the bombers came over the village. A moment later came the long whistle of the first bomb.

I counted up to forty-three bombs before I lost count. The militia officer with me counted up to sixty.

Huge columns of black smoke and a spurt of flame here and there arose around us, and through it the terrible hopeless wailing of the babies and the trembling voices of their peasant mothers trying to comfort them.

I saw a girl of fifteen to twenty years of age run by, her hands spread out on her breasts, her head thrown back, and her eyes staring madly at nothing. She stumbled wildly forward with little harsh sobs across the ploughed land, out of her wits from the bombing, running crazily nowhere in particular.

We picked ourselves out of the dung heap into which we unfortunately had to throw ourselves, and drove on towards Madrid.

The bombers had got as far as the northern edge of Cuatro Caminos before the government chasers met them and drove them off. There they had emptied a cargo of bombs into a densely packed huddle of little one and two-storey working-class houses just outside the main road.

There must have been at least a dozen families, probably more, in those houses. When we got there they were a heap of rubble in which the neighbours dug furiously among the wreckage. The whole street was thick with debris and ambulances, and stretcher-bearers tore to and fro.

It has not yet been possible to establish the total number of dead and wounded.

Daily Worker, 23 December 1936

BRITONS TO FORM 2 COMPANIES?

Famous Regiment Dissolves Itself, Enters New Army

MADRID, Tuesday.
It looks as though within a very short time there will be not one but two all-British companies in the International Brigade.

This fine news comes within a week of the first announcement of the formation of the first all-British company.

That announcement was greeted with the greatest possible satisfaction by the other members of the Brigades and by the Spanish fighters whom the volunteers of the Brigades are helping in the defence of Madrid.

There is now hardly a sector of the Madrid front where front-line fighters of the Republic have not seen at first-hand the excellence of those two groups of Englishmen who have been fighting partly in one of the French companies and partly in one of the German.

There will be real enthusiasm here at the news that the anti-fascists of Britain have been rallying to the defence of Europe against Fascism to such good purpose that the announcement of the formation of a second British company is already in sight.

At the moment all the British members of the Brigade are at the base camp helping to plan and organise the new volunteers.

In a ceremony as significant as it was impressive, the famous Fifth Regiment yesterday formally renounced its separate existence and incorporated itself in the regular brigades of the new army.

The history of the Fifth Regiment, from its birth on 27 July is the history of the development of the People's Army. The Fifth Regiment was brought into existence in July, when the Communist Party recognised the need for a force different in kind and in basis from the militia groups.

It took the step then considered almost eccentric of putting 200 men through a special training and made of them the basis of the Steel Companies, without which the enemy would have forced the sierra front by mid-August.

Yesterday, the Fifth Regiment was able to announce that it has on the front no less than 60,000 men, every one of whom has received, at any rate, the elements of a military and political training.

The voluntary merging of its forces in the organisation of the People's Army is the Communist Party's way of putting into practice the proposals of unification and militarisation contained in the great manifesto issued a few days ago. This has been and will continue to be the focal point of all political discussions here for a long time to come.

I had the honour to be present on the occasion when, under the blazing sun of August, the Steel Battalion of the Fifth Regiment was drawn up on the Square at Cuatro Caminos to receive from the Italian Communist Party the flag under which that Party fought in the first struggles against Italian Fascism.

For years this relic had been treasured by the illegal fighters against Fascism. In August they presented it to the Steel Battalion as being men worthy to keep and fight under it.

Yesterday, the Fifth Regiment handed over that banner to be one of the standards of the new unified People's Army of Spain.

Daily Worker, 1 January 1937

PASIONARIA LAUGHS AT HER OWN 'DEATH'

VALENCIA, Thursday.
A deep chuckling laugh was audible all through the offices of the Communist Party here this afternoon when I told Dolores

Pasionaria that the London newspapers at that moment were publishing the news of her death, complete with photograph.

The laugh was Pasionaria's. 'You don't say?' she said. 'Looks like those people really are anxious about having me dead. That is the third time I have been dead in England in this war alone.'

I reminded her that when I was here in 1934 I had twice had the job of asking her the same question for the same reason, namely whether she would confirm the London newspapers' account of her death.

She started to laugh again. 'Well,' she said, 'Tell them I'm alive and kicking.' She paused. 'Mind you get that – and kicking!'

'And tell them that when Franco's dead and Mola's dead and Queipo de Llano's dead, I shall start perhaps to think about dying, too.

'And tell them as they don't seem to know it yet, that all those generals have arms a darned sight too short to get me – a darned sight too short.'

Still laughing, she rushed out of the room on another job in her eternally busy day as the accepted leader of the honest and decent women of Spain in their struggle against the enslavement and degradation of Fascism.

Daily Worker, 4 January 1937

BRITISH BATTALION IN ACTION

Franco Checked In
South Spain Battles

MADRID, Sunday.
The most important news of the weekend is, first, the application amid general approval of a government decree 'militarising' the war industries throughout the country in all government-controlled territory.

Full details of what this will mean in practice are not available.

The main point of the decree is that all factories already

producing, or considered as suitable to produce all kinds of war material – which, of course, includes factories producing material for military transport, military supplies, etc. – will be under direct military control.

Other factories will not be permitted to enter into war production.

The decree is the beginning of a real rationalisation of production in relation to war needs.

It is a long step towards putting into effect one of the most important of the proposals listed a few weeks ago in the famous manifesto issued by the Communist Party of Spain, entitled 'The Road to Victory', a publication which may truthfully be said to mark the turning-point of this war.

The second big news of the weekend comes from the Córdoba front. The Republican forces are checking the first rush of the enemy advance towards the wealthy mining area north-east of Córdoba – the area centred around Linarca. A counter-attack has proved successful at a number of points.

The check to the enemy advance on this front is the more remarkable as it signifies an enormously accelerated rate of progress in the militarisation of the Republican forces in the south.

As I have repeatedly said, everything now depends on the rate of efficient militarisation of the Republican forces – the rate, that is to say, at which the new army can be turned into efficient infantry.

The process has been going on at Madrid, under the guidance of the Fifth Regiment and under the pressure of the Communist Party.

Here, already, we have for many weeks seen infantry forces developing out of the rawest militia who started the war with nothing but their courage and enthusiasm to help them through.

Now the same process has reached the Córdoba front.

No one who saw, as I did, the condition of that front last August, can fail to understand what tremendous organisational and political work has been carried out.

By it the Republican forces have been brought into a condition where they are capable of meeting, checking and, in some places, of actually throwing back an enemy attack on which Franco has concentrated many of his best forces and his highest hopes.

For Englishmen there will be an especial pride and interest in the news from this front. It is here that the first forces of the newly formed all-British Battalion are in action.

Haldane Unhurt By Gas

MADRID, Sunday.

Having breakfasted this morning with Professor J.B.S. Haldane, I can assure all those who have been anxious about his state of health that the Professor is in the most excellent spirits and only suffering from a severe cough and huskiness.

Commenting on the prominence given in the British press to news of his mishap during an experiment with poison gas, he said, 'There is, however, one very interesting side to all this. Everyone can see that there is enormous interest in England in the whole question of anti-gas defence. People want to hear the latest about the experiences of Madrid in this matter and of course, as we all know, experiments are continually being made in London.

'But what I cannot understand is why the London County Council, which, as a Labour LCC, is certainly profoundly interested in every possible means of improving the anti-gas defences of the working millions of London, does not send out some experts here to observe the work of the Republican authorities of Madrid.'

Daily Worker, 12 January 1937

REBELS SUFFER HUGE LOSSES

MADRID, Monday.

After the quiet which continued on all fronts throughout the greater part of the day, reports from the front late this afternoon suggest that by tonight the second stage of the greatest battle of the war will be getting under way.

Thick mist all across the Madrid tableland has put the aeroplanes on the ground. There is a feeling, however, that the enemy have by now got over the temporary disorder which the unexpected resistance and the colossal losses they suffered in the first drive have caused. It is thought that the enemy losses in the last week must have been four times our own.

The compulsory evacuation of something between a quarter and half a million people from this city, under order from the Defence Council, is now going into effect.

The normal population of Madrid was around one million. Refugees from invaded areas have held that number to – probably – a million and a half. By this new order for compulsory evacuation all those families not engaged in war work the Defence Council have undertaken the biggest task that has faced any government since the last German invasion of the rest of Europe.

This task that will become history is rapidly to evacuate one-third of the population of Vargo and arrange for them to be distributed and cared for in various villages and principal districts out of reach of attack by German bombers.

For weeks an attempt has been made to put the object of this order into effect, and upwards of a quarter of a million have already been got out of the city in this way, but there are still scores of thousands of people who cannot bring themselves to leave their homes and their possessions even though by staying where they are they run considerable danger of losing their lives. But they must be evacuated as, by remaining where they are, they are enormously and needlessly complicating the problem of feeding those who have to be there.

It is an extraordinary fact that there are thousands of people who have been bombed from one village after another, who have seen their refuge in Madrid blown to pieces, and who yet are unwilling to move themselves, even to the other side of the same city.

On Sunday afternoon you could see them with their children in their arms, standing about in the devastated western portion of the city looking for the wreckage of their old home and retrieving some small pieces of furniture or clothing from them. These are the people who are now being compulsorily evacuated in batches of fifty to places of comparative security and plenty.

It is understood that the most effective means of solving this urgent and overdue problem will be the refusal of food tickets to people who insist on trying to remain here without being engaged on war work.

Chapter Three

FROM MÁLAGA TO THE FOREIGN BAN

After an interval in London in January 1937, Cockburn returned to Spain and was able to reach Málaga, then becoming the most important area on the southern front. He reports the fall of the city after Italian air attack and the reinforcement of the Nationalist forces by Italy in the south, then travels north to cover the struggle for Oviedo and the Battle of Guadalajara.

Daily Worker, 6 February 1937

FIRST STORY FROM MÁLAGA FRONT

Pitcairn Runs Gauntlet Of Bombers

Frank Pitcairn, our Special Correspondent in Spain, has added to his long series of brilliant exploits in the civil war by being the first to cover the Málaga battle-front.

Achieving this feat, he ran the gauntlet of Italian bombers while motoring along the narrow coast road exposed to enemy fire.

The despatch of this, his first message, was delayed by the fact that the car which was conveying it to the cable station was caught by an enemy bomber and suffered a cracked cylinder.

MÁLAGA, Friday.

Six hours before I got into Málaga, I thought that Málaga would fall. Now I doubt it.

When we saw the place lying in the distance on the narrow beach between the sea and the sierras somebody said, 'We may get into this place, but we shan't get out of it alive.'

I thought then the speaker was probably right. That was before I had visited the Málaga fronts.

On the way we had seen villages where at night people go into the fields to sleep for fear of being killed in bed by bombs. That is what Europe has come to.

The road we passed along was covered with straggling caravans of refugees.

Málaga lies at the end of it like the last western outpost of civilised Europe. Also, it lies at the foot of two others running south to north.

This war is fought on roads – being the most highly mechanised war yet seen. Roads are more vital than ever.

The rebel push for Málaga is a push for roads. Particularly for roads running north direct from a suitable landing place for German and Italian troops.

At Vélez de Málaga further east, and further east again at Motril, two other roads run north from the main east-west road. They cut the otherwise impassable sierras – huge bulging deserts squeezing the coast plain in most cases to breadth of a few score yards and rising barrenly from clusters of almond trees at their base to heavy snow caps on top.

Westward, the low ground broadens out into a widish strip of coast land – maybe half a mile – rising gently into low, sharp, peaked hills, these rising in turn to rocky sierras.

The front runs from just east of Marbella up to the east of Alora, turns eastwards again and runs south of Antequera through Alfarnate on the Granada road, bending then south-eastwards to a point about thirteen miles due north of Motril.

Particularly at Motril, Vélez de Málaga, and between Málaga and Marbella, there is a considerable flat coast land covered mostly with sugar cane and maize.

Thus the Marbella front is probable the most difficult to hold.

I spent most of yesterday morning in the furthest outposts of that sub-sector. A Political Commissar who is a member of the Left Republicans showed me round.

Only a few weeks ago, the troops on this front – then quiet and restful – were composed of various political columns each representing one single political party. Today all that is altered.

The columns are now one coherent military force.

Under pressure of the German-Italian attack the columns were formed into battalions and brigades, which at first consisted of smaller units still composed exclusively of the members of one party.

In the course of battle experience these differences were deliberately merged by the men themselves.

The fact is that the militarisation of the army which in the rest of Spain was a process of gradual development, lasting from the end of August to the end of January, in Andalucía has been a quite sudden affair, only starting a few weeks ago, but already very far advanced.

In the Hotel Caleta Palace, at Málaga, which was the grandest luxury hotel of the city and much frequented by British people rich enough to go south for the winter, hangs a map showing 'short excursions', and another showing 'longer excursions'.

The first is supposed to show places you could go to between reading the *Morning Post* after breakfast and drinking the first cocktail before lunch.

There is no single point of the present front which is not on the 'short excursion' list.

Six weeks ago a big enemy drive might have gone through that happy-go-lucky front like paper. That is not so today.

It is estimated that the rebels have to keep twelve or fourteen thousand men on that front. More significant still, the forces on the Málaga front at Marbella have shown themselves capable of swift and determined advance.

The advanced company headquarters I was in yesterday was in rebel territory only a fortnight back, following the first big rebel drive which took Estepona and swept forward through Marbella towards Fuengirola.

A new push is just beginning. It may – with all the weight of German and Italian arms and men behind it – bring the rebel lines forward again, but it will be faced with a very different and very much more exhausting resistance than anything seen on the Málaga front before.

Daily Worker, 8 February 1937

RACING AGAINST DEATH

Epic Courage Of 'The Belgians Of The War'

VALENCIA, Sunday.

When the church bells ring in Málaga that means the Italian and German aeroplanes are coming over. While I was there they came twice and three times a day. The horror of the civilian bombing is even worse in Málaga than in Madrid. The place is so small and so terribly exposed.

When the bells begin ringing and you see people who have been working in the harbour or in the market place, or elsewhere in the open, run in crowds, you know that they are literally running a race against death.

But the houses in Málaga are mostly low and rather flimsy, and without cellars. Where the cliffs come down to the edge of the town, the people make for the rocks and caves in which those who can reach them take refuge. Others rush bounding up the hillside above the town.

Those in the town, with an air of infinite weariness, wait behind the piles of sandbags which have been set up in front of the doorways of the apartment blocks. Though they are not safe from bombs falling on the houses, they are relatively protected from an explosion in the street and from the bullets of the machine-guns.

Sometimes you can see the aeroplane machine-gunner working the gun as the plane swoops along above the street.

If you were to imagine, however, that this terribly hammered town is in a state of panic you would be wrong. Nothing I have seen in this war has impressed me more than the power of the Spanish people's resistance to attack than the attitude of the people as seen in Málaga.

Exposed there at the end of that long single track narrow road between the mountains and the sea, they are very clearly conscious of their role as being the last outpost of Spain under the combined attack of two foreign powers.

One man said to me, 'We are the Belgians of this war.' They read and discuss day after day and week after week news of the, to them, utterly incomprehensible attitude of the British government.

The sudden urgent clang of the alarm bell time and again interrupts the eager reading of the despatches from London, Paris and Geneva.

I was myself the eye-witness a couple of days ago of an episode which might serve as a microcosm of the battle in Málaga. We were driving between the hills just outside Nerja, some miles east of Málaga.

Cliffs dropped away precipitously to the water's edge. Two hundred yards out, aground in the shallow water in the big rocks, you could see the wrecked *Dolphin*, which had been bringing food supplies to the civilian population of Málaga.

First it was bombed by Italian aeroplanes, then, as the captain made for the shore, it was torpedoed by a submarine, either German or Italian, for the rebels have none of their own. As we passed she lay there with a huge hole torn in her side by the torpedo and marks of the bombs on her sides.

Suddenly, as we rounded the curve of the main road, above the ship we saw a huge Italian aeroplane, accompanied by two pursuit planes, roaring up from the south. At the same time there appeared far out to sea the conning tower of a submarine emerging slowly. We had time to jump from the car by the side of the road and run fifty yards into the rocks before the first bomb fell between the road and the sea.

Two peasant carts were coming, full of women and babies and household belongings, refugees from Málaga. We shouted to them to get off the road quick. They stood gaping uncertainly for a moment at the strange aeroplanes. Then, as another bomb fell, this time near the ship, they began awkwardly to run, stumbling back along the road towards a deep culvert.

With the aerial monster swooping close over them, the women with their babies climbed down under cover of the stonework. When the tiny refuge was full the men started to run up towards the hill.

Nine times while the submarine watched from the sea and the chaser planes circled slowly above, the bomber turned above the stricken *Dolphin*/

We had found a place where we could lie over the end of a fairly protective projection of rock. We saw one bomb fall almost on top of our car, and the next one sent a sudden column of white smoke soaring up from approximately the same spot. It began to look as though we should have to walk home.

The whole thing lasted about twenty minutes. Suddenly, without our being able to see why, we saw the enemy chasers dash towards the shore and the machine-gunner of the big bomber standing up working his gun. Then we knew that the government pursuit planes had arrived from Málaga.

For another fifteen minutes there raged close above our heads an aerial battle, of which we could only get glimpses, with a stream of machine-gun bullets cutting close beside us.

Part of the time we could see the chasers sweeping between the peaks of rock, part of the time we could only see their shadows chasing one another at terrific speed across the sunny grass.

A machine-gun bullet hit one of the oxen; the team stampeded, the cart with all the people's belongings in it was dragged over the edge of the road and tumbled in the rocks.

The horses of the other cart stood solidly unmoving through it all, although from where we were the force of the bombs was sufficient to scatter pieces of rock over us.

At the end of it all the bomber, flying very low, tore for the south with the pursuit planes close behind it. The submarine submerged, the government chasers circled watchfully and then made off towards Málaga.

The women and children came out from the culvert, all the babies crying loudly and the older women crying softly, the men cursing the Germans and Italians as they looked at their ruined cart.

Daily Worker, 9 February 1937

REBELS DESERT ON MÁLAGA FRONT

Jump Train When Cultivated Fields Appear

VALENCIA, Monday.

Just beyond the north sector of the Málaga front the railway goes through the mountains towards Granada. East of

Antequera last week a man jumped from a train as it slowed up on a mountain curve, lay hidden in the rocks for a couple of hours until darkness, came stumbling through the boulders and water courses to the government positions in front of Alfernate.

He was a policeman from Seville – escaping into loyal territory. They asked him how he and others – for this has happened fairly often before – knew just exactly when to jump the train, always at the point nearest our lines. He explained immediately.

'Because', he said, 'we keep a lookout from the train, all the time watching to see a place to the south where the fields and the olive groves on the hillsides are properly cultivated.

'In the rebel territory, you understand everything is desert. Nobody works in the fields any more. So when you look up into the hills from the train and see the fields in order and people working in them you know that is where the government territory begins and you jump.'

I talked to a lot of deserters down in Malaga and they all of them say about the same thing. The queerest of the lot was a Hungarian, who had come across the day before on the Marbella front.

He was a good-looking young fellow and a powerful liar. He was, according to himself, a deserter who had intended to desert right from the outset – he said he had only joined up on the other side because he happened to be in Gibraltar on a British ship as a stowaway from Marseilles and he had been turned out of Gibraltar and gone to La Linea, where, he said, he had joined up with the Fascists so as to be able to run across to the government lines as quickly as possible.

When we investigated him it turned out that only about fifteen per cent of his story was true. But at the same time it was equally evident that although he had lied to us, he was not a spy.

On the contrary, he was a typical exhibit among thousands of the sort of wretched, neurotic, beaten-down young men, penniless, hopeless, stupid, licked and a trifle loose in the head, whom today rebel agents all over Europe are shipping into rebel territory to fight for the Fascists, who find they can get no support among their own people.

He came from a village in Hungary, where he had helped in his father's carpenter's shop. Like all Hungarian villages at this time, the place was more than half-starved. For that reason and because, it seems, of the hopelessness of it all and because perhaps he was already a trifle dotty, he committed some sort of a crime there – just what it was he wouldn't, even at the end of three hours' fairly drastic interrogation, tell us.

So he left the village without a passport and wandered about doing odd jobs in Austria and Switzerland and finally, after passing through Munich and smuggling himself somehow across the French frontier and into Morocco, got picked up by Fascist recruiting agents in Oran and was shipped from there to Gibraltar and from there to La Linea. There he joined the Falange, and after two days on the Marbella front, slipped across the lines to join the government troops.

The two facts of especial interest he revealed – apart from the general facts of the sort of man who gets caught up these days in the Fascist war machine – were first, that he was definitely assisted to live in Gibraltar by the British authorities there, while awaiting his enrolment in Franco's forces, and second, that there is in Gibraltar itself an actual recruiting station for such people run by an Hungarian.

On the Málaga front deserters come over at the rate of anything from a dozen to thirty a day. The odd thing is they come over even when things are going very badly for us and very well for the rebels. One man – a Spaniard – who had come across like that was asked why he did so.

His answer was interesting: 'I am the son of a shopkeeper, and my mother was an olive gatherer and there are more shopkeepers and olive gatherers on this side than there are with Fascists. So here I am.'

Daily Worker, 10 February 1937

CITY CRUSHED BY NAZI AND ITALIAN ARMS

New Phase of Invasion

VALENCIA, Tuesday.
Málaga has fallen. The crumpled front now runs somewhere east of Vélez de Málaga, across the Almería road.

Rebel warships, escorted by German submarines, are bombing the single road to Almería. The road is jammed with refugees, on foot and in carts. In parts it is literally as crowded as the road to Wembley on a Cup-Tie day. In some places shells have bitten out chunks of rock on the road, and reduced it to a mere track between the precipices.

In Málaga the German and Italian troops, whose sudden arrival on this front have made the thing possible, are celebrating, while the Falangists proceed with the systematic massacre of 40,000 people, maybe more.

The desert of Fascist territory has again been pushed forward a long way into civilised Europe.

It is of the gravest importance that the people of England should understand why and how this has happened so suddenly and so quickly.

As the only British journalist to have visited all the Málaga fronts just before the disaster, and one of only five foreign journalists who have been in Málaga at all this year, I can perhaps speak with some authority on a matter which is, or should be, the urgent concern of the remains of democratic Europe.

It was the opinion, not only of myself but of every competent observer who saw the Málaga front last week, that the enemy drive of a few weeks before had not only been held, but that the initiative was definitely passing to the government side.

I spent hours walking over the ground on all the fronts and discussed the position with people who had fought there throughout, and with others newly arrived, but with expert military knowledge.

I talked also with many deserters – from whom we had a fairly full picture of conditions on the other side. They were extremely bad. The consensus of opinion was absolute that the enemy army, as it stood, could not take Málaga. It was perfectly clear that nothing short of a foreign invasion on a scale far surpassing anything yet seen in Spain would break through.

There had been Italian and German troops on that front, but they had failed. The question-mark which hung over everything was this: Have the Germans and Italians already landed enough regulars to form a full-size invading army, and if so, will the international situation permit them to use them?

Today we have the answer to both these questions. I remember well how in the General Staff Headquarters in

Málaga on Monday night we discussed reports from the Paris press of the landing of the Italian troops and German troops, and particularly the landing of more than 100 Italian planes.

There were several among those present who did not believe these reports or, at least, thought them very much exaggerated.

I confess that I thought myself the figures were probably too high. I know that there are a very large number of people in England who, just as we did in Málaga, still think that the extent and character of the foreign invasion of Spain is being exaggerated.

That is why I think it is important to tell you this. Because I know now, and every single person who has been in Málaga this year, knows that the figures were not exaggerated, and that the real invasion has only just begun.

With the attack on Málaga, in which German and Italian Infantry, German and Italian tanks, German and Italian aeroplanes and German and Italian warships all took part – it is admitted in Gibraltar that Queipo de Llano watched the proceedings from the deck of a German cruiser – the war of invasion has entered a new phase.

The troops were rushed in immediately following the British government's control proposal, and the measures taken by Britain and France to prevent the sending of volunteers to fight for Spain.

Now they have struck their first big blow. Shelled from the sea, bombarded from the air and machine-gunned from the biggest fleet of tanks seen in this war, the government infantry were faced with an infantry attack by German troops, wearing not only the new steel helmets of the Reichswehr, but also the new steel cuirass, or breastplate, and using the new hand grenades, manufactured by Krupp, which fly into seven pieces in the air, each of which explodes separately as it hits the ground.

In a week everything has changed. A week ago at Málaga it was clear that if the Germans and Italians did not invade – in other words, if the alleged object of British policy were to be realised – then the attack on Málaga would fail.

The attack has succeeded precisely because the German and Italian governments paid no more attention to proposals for control than they have to previous proposals.

With that the whole alleged basis of the policy of the last two weeks is exploded. It is not a question of report and supposition. It is a fact which is being paid for in rivers of blood in the streets of Málaga today.

Democratic Europe has been fooled again. As a result it has lost a great city. That is the ugly, unanswerable fact which faces the shuffling and the hypocrisy of Baldwin diplomacy.

Daily Worker, 11 February 1937

SPAIN'S ANSWER TO MÁLAGA

People Ask 'What Will Britain Do?'

VALENCIA, Wednesday.

'The answer to a defeat is a victory and a half,' this is the slogan which Alvarez del Vayo, the High Commissioner for War, has given to Republican Spain on the occasion of the fall of Málaga.

The loss of Málaga is freely recognised as a very heavy blow. It is a good sign of the tougher fibre of the Republicans that on this occasion the government and the War Commissioner have spoken openly of the gravity of what has happened – a sign of trust in the determination and tenacity of the people in welcome contrast to some of the defeatist tendencies which surrounded the retreat up the Tagus Valley last year when the Germans first started sending war materials en masse.

Today the air is electric with the realisation – supported by the admission of the British press – that now, an open, unconcealed war of intervention on a grand scale has begun.

The man in the street knows today that the Italo-German attack is not only an attack by means of war materials, officers, experts and occasional cadres of troops, supplied from Rome and Berlin but an invasion in the complete sense of the word.

Everyone understands that with this the whole situation of Spain and of Europe has undergone a profound change. Spain stands ready to dig in its heels and fight to the last man for its independence.

But while it prepared for the most terrific struggle of the whole war, Spain – the soldier on the front, the clerk in the office, the worker in the factory, the housewife and the statesman, the Communist, the Liberal and the Socialist – is asking:

'What is democratic Europe going to do now? And above all: What will Britain do?'

'Latest Chapter Of Brutal Intervention'

VALENCIA, Wednesday.

The charge that a chief cause of the fall of Málaga was the intervention of two Italian battleships is made in a detailed statement issued after a long session by the Council of Ministers.

The statement, which was made public by Jesús Hernández, Minister of Public Education and Secretary of the Council, is as follows:

'On 7 February, at 10 a.m., three destroyers left the Republican naval base of Cartagena, in order to give battle to the rebel cruisers *Baleares, Canarias* and the *Almirante Cervera*, which had been bombarding the Málaga coast.

'At 1.50 p.m., as the Republican ships advanced carefully, in order to avoid foreign submarines in their path, they sighted two cruisers, south of Cape Gata, which they took to be the cruisers *Canarias* and *Baleares*.

'The ships manoeuvred elaborately in order to lead the Republican ships away from the spot where the real insurgent cruisers were operating. When the distance between the two lines of ships had been sufficiently narrowed, the Republican vessels were able by their searchlights to ascertain that in front of them were two Italian battleships, the *Muzio Artendolo* and the *Armando Dia*.

'Such latitude on the part of neutral vessels is without precedent in world naval history. Evidently the Italian ships planned to eliminate the Republican ships from the battle, to reduce their stocks of fuel and to scatter the Republican forces.'

The conduct of the two Italian ships, continues the statement, is yet another outrage, following upon the action of German battleships in laying mines along the coast of Cantabria; the spying on the Republican fleet carried out by German and Italian battleships in the Mediterranean, and the night attacks by the foreign ships on the Spanish coast.

'Ever since last September, the government of the Republic has incessantly denounced from the highest international tribunes, and by many appeals to the Powers subscribing to the Non-Intervention Agreement, the outrageous infractions of international law by Germany and Italy.

'Those who have received the news of the fall of Málaga as a sign of weakening of the Republican side and might be inclined to see in it a step towards the end of the war, are entirely mistaken.

'The only consequence the fall of Málaga can have for the government and for the Spanish people who elected and support it is a still stronger determination not to give way in the fight until the final victory is gained.

'Foreign intervention does not shorten the war. It makes the war longer and more intense, at the same time bringing Europe still more closely to the precipice.'

A denial that the Madrid-Valencia road is cut has been made by the Madrid Defence Committee.

Yesterday, their statement says the road was under shell-fire near the River Jarama, but in the afternoon operations ceased.

Vallecas, the southern suburb of Madrid, was also yesterday subjected to a severe bombardment by artillery and from the air.

On other fronts the Republican forces successfully replied to insurgent offensives. No change in the fronts took place.

Daily Worker, 17 February 1937

ITALY RUSHING MEN TO MÁLAGA

German Guns Point At You

New and damning proof of German and Italian flouting of 'non-intervention'; of open Fascist preparation for European war; of British government complaisance which means in fact aid for the warmakers – all this is given in the amazing message our correspondent, Frank Pitcairn, sends from Gibraltar.

GIBRALTAR, Tuesday.
Of the two key-points of the Spanish war, one is Madrid and the other is right here in and around the Straits of Gibraltar. Here you can see the war of intervention in being. Here are the facts. They are in possession of every intelligence service operating round here.

Queipo de Llano's next move is held up because he is awaiting more Italian troops from Italy. They will disembark at Málaga. Messages from further east report that a ship of the Italian line, which usually carries troops, is already within a few hours' sail of Málaga.

Incidentally, I learned from deserters that the same line has regularly conveyed Spanish rebel troops between the Balearic Islands and Cadiz, thus covering their movements under the cloak of 'neutrality'.

The total number of Italian troops landed at Cadiz during the last two months is not more than 42,000, and not less than 37,000.

All these were taken by train from Cadiz to Jerez de la Frontera. In this way we have a double check on the numbers – one from the watchers on the port, and the other from the road and rail junction.

From Jerez the troops are distributed directly to the front. That point is important and should be noted. There is no question of training camps for them. They arrive under their own battalion and company officers and go straight into the line.

In other words, the pretence that these are volunteers and not regular troops falls to the ground the moment you know their timetables.

Full reports now available give the number arriving at Cadiz in two days – and only two days – before the final drive against Málaga as between 13,000 and 15,000. They went straight into the line and took Málaga. 13,000 Italian regulars against the militia!

When the British government signed the 'Gentlemen's Agreement', the Italians were understood to have made a big gesture in withdrawing the notorious Count Rossi from the Balearic Islands. This was supposed to be a sign that they were pulling out from intervention. And we were sold again. Rossi is now in Seville. The Seville newspaper *Correo de Andalucía* of 14 February openly refers to his presence there.

Upholders of the present non-intervention policy declare that it is at least preventing the spread of war, hoping thus to scare the democrats into acceptance of the situation. The facts tell a different story.

I have been in Tangier and am now in Gibraltar. The facts are that the Germans and Italians are quite openly using the present situation as a jumping-off point for war which will put your houses in London and Glasgow in the same danger as the houses of Madrid and Valencia.

Tangier and Gibraltar are not only in the middle of this war, they are already half-way into the next.

Here you can see the warmakers at work. Three days ago, on Saturday, they landed at Algeciras 215 German military engineers and artillery officers.

For about four miles south of Algeciras the coast runs approximately due south and then turns and runs south-west for about another fourteen miles to Morocco Point and Tarrifa. That strip of coast faces and is nearest to the coast of Spanish Morocco – from Ceuta to the Tangier border.

When the present war broke out the strip on the Spanish side up to Tarrifa was fortified with a few batteries, with old, small guns.

Two months ago the old batteries were suddenly scrapped and new ones established. Trials were then carried out to see whether these in combination with the new batteries of Ceuta were sufficient to give absolute command of the Straits.

The trials proved unsatisfactory, the batteries on the Spanish side being not powerful enough.

The job of this latest batch of engineers and artillerymen is to carry out a second reorganisation of the batteries in fortification.

Why? The point is that the sole possible purpose of such batteries is aggression against shipping in the Straits. The only defensive purpose could be the defence of Algeciras, for which the old batteries are perfectly sufficient.

Nobody even pretends that these new batteries are for defensive purposes. They are perfectly open preparation for European war, for the closing of the Straits.

When similar preparations were revealed in Spanish Morocco and the French government took strong action, the French Right press denounced the whole thing as a wicked rumour. The Germans declared 'All quiet'. Now the same thing is happening on the northern side.

Challenge the German government to permit a mixed commission, representing the French People's Front, the French government, the British government and the British opposition parties to visit the coast west of Tarrifa.

The Commission find there a high explosive proof that Germany is preparing war, and war soon; and using the present policy of the British and French governments as an ideal backing for the preparations which threaten us all.

The German cruiser *Deutschland*, with scouting planes clearly visible on her decks, is still here. The second battalion of the Gordon Highlanders supplied a guard of honour to Rear-Admiral Fischel when he came to pay a call on the Governor of Gibraltar. The streets are full of German sailors, marching about at night singing the Horst-Wessel song as they do at Cadiz. The *Deutschland* arrived here from Cadiz.

I am able to confirm that some German warship invariably accompanies the Spanish rebel vessels when they leave the port.

The German authorities have just offered the managership of mining concessions in Spanish Morocco, which they acquired as new sources of war material, to an American financier who is engaged to the daughter of General Mola.

I have just seen a horrible photograph of rebel troops after 'cleaning up' a village in the Málaga advance. There are fifteen men standing posed in line like a football team. Four of them are carrying the severed and still bleeding heads of dead government supporters massacred by them.

Daily Worker, 18 February 1937

'FIRST ACT OF THE WORLD WAR'

Militia Doctor Sees What Eden Ignores

MADRID, Wednesday.

'That is the stage on which the first act of the world war drama is being played,' said a doctor of the militia to me today, pointing down to the Valley of the Jarama as we lay on a hill in long, thyme-scented grass.

I had driven out from Madrid along the Valencia road, turning off along a mule track about ten miles from the city. The track carried us into the heart of the hills, along whose seemingly deserted slopes reverberated the booming of guns.

At last we came to a little hollow in whose shelter stood two ambulance cars.

'This is the place,' said the army doctor with me, and getting out he told us to follow. Imitating my guide, I crawled up the slope to the summit and there we lay prone with our nostrils buried in the thyme and our eyes fixed on the field of battle.

This was Valley of the Jarama, that stream whose name, beside that of the Manzanares, is now being written with letters of blood in imperishable annals of humanity's fight for liberty. Beyond the stream were our lines facing the long forbidding ridge of Redondo, now held by enemy.

A week ago, in the most powerful drive since the battle for Madrid began, the rebels advanced along the ridge, and now from the bluff at the northern end their fire commands the Valencia road and compels the convoys of lorries carrying precious food to Madrid to make a detour to the north.

But the mercenary troops of international Fascism, despite repeated attempts, have not yet set their feet on the road; between them and their goal stand the men of the young Republican Army, determined that just as the Manzanares defied Franco when he tried to storm Madrid, so shall the Jarama defy him as he tries to starve it.

Through field-glasses we could see bands of rebel troops move along the ridge.

'This morning we saw a priest among them,' said the doctor. 'He was carrying a machine-gun, but as soon as our men opened fire he scurried off and took cover behind a boulder. Most of his companions over there seem to be Moors.

'At night the Moors steal down the hillside and crawl towards our lines. Then, when they are quite near, they jump up, and uttering fiendish cries to frighten our men, rush forward. But our lads are not frightened, and in many cases those wild cries of the Moors have been their last.'

A mule with two stretchers strapped to its saddle was grazing in the hollow.

'That's how we bring in our wounded,' the doctor explained. 'Two men at a time. They have to be carried across the bridge which spans the Jarama and up this side of the valley to where we are, all under enemy fire.

'Today we have brought in between sixty and seventy. Ten were dead.'

Seriously wounded men, if they survive that nightmare ride on the mule across the valley of death, are treated in one of the ambulances which are equipped with an operating-table.

There in that hollow among the hills, sometimes with shells falling all around and machine-gun bullets flying overhead, always with the sound of the guns in their ears, surgeons risked their own lives to save a comrade's.

Afterwards the wounded were transferred to another ambulance and driven along the mule track to the main road, and so to Madrid.

Remember that these men who suffer the agony of such an experience could all have escaped it had they liked.

They joined the militia of their own will, and last October, when the militia were militarised, they were given the chance to quit.

It is only now after seven months of the war that the cry for compulsory military service has been raised.

Another doctor joined us on the hillside. It was he who made the remark I have quoted at the beginning of this article.

'It beats me', he said, 'how people in England and France seem to be blind to the issue that is at stake here.

'Señor Eden, for instance, doesn't he realise what the fall of Málaga means, not for us here in Spain – though that is bad enough – but for the British?'

The guns on both sides of the hill began to bark again, and we heard the drone of war planes. Afterwards we were told of a battle in which three rebel planes were brought crashing down in flames.

In Italy or Germany three more families would soon be mourning the loss of sons sacrificed on the altar of Fascist imperialism.

Daily Worker, 27 February 1937

OUR REPORTER ON MINED LINER

Italian Submarine Suspected

PORT-VENDRES (FRANCE), Friday.
The 10,000 ton *Llandovery Castle* liner, outward bound from London to East and South African ports, is today lying in Port-Vendres, five miles from the Spanish frontier, with her port side ripped open by one of the mines broadcast through these

waters by rebel minelayers trying to blockade Barcelona.

The boat was mined about fourteen miles south-east of here at 4.45 yesterday evening, and finally – sinking fast by the bows – ran into shallow water off Port-Vendres bathing beach just after dawn this morning.

There were no casualties. Twice the boat escaped by the merest chance a disaster which would have meant sudden death to at least several score of its crew and passengers.

Having spent a considerable part of the night on the bridge of the *Llandovery Castle* as interpreter between the British officers and the French who came to the rescue, I was able to get a somewhat fuller picture of what really happened than the majority of passengers, many of whom were unaware of the full extent of the danger until it was all over.

I had been warned by British officers at Gibraltar that the rebels, with the assistance of Italian trawlers, were believed to be recklessly throwing mines about between the Balearic Islands and the Franco-Spanish border.

The *Llandovery Castle* was off the Franco-Spanish frontier, and on the last lap of the trip to Marseilles when there were sighted almost simultaneously two black objects in the water close by – one which looked like a floating football, the other like a bottle floating upright.

The first was a mine, the second, in the opinion of the First Officer, was probably, though not certainly, the periscope of an enemy submarine.

A moment later another mine struck the ship on the port side of the forward hold. There was an explosion, which blew the heavy forward hatches high into the air, sent a column of water over the decks, wrecked two cabins, completely tearing the fittings from the wall and filled the whole ship with the acrid smell of burning cordite.

If the mine had struck a matter of two or three yards further forward it would quite certainly have killed a score of the crew, who were then in their quarters.

As it was, the hold where it struck was full of cement and cork – one could hardly imagine a more fortunate cargo from the point of view of blocking the mine.

A moment after the explosion, when fortunately the majority of those on board were only intent on preparations for leaving the ship, another mine – probably coupled with the one which exploded, appeared on the starboard side of the ship.

If it had exploded the ship would probably have gone down in a few minutes. As it was, this mine passed without damage.

Even so, at the rate the water was coming in, it looked for a while as if the ship would have to be abandoned immediately.

The boats were swung out and stocked with provisions, and the passengers and crew stood ready with their lifebelts on.

The behaviour of three somewhat mysterious craft in the neighbourhood added to the impression of the officers that the bottle-like object we had seen was in fact the periscope of a submarine.

Two small boats, apparently trawlers, which had been coming out from the shore, turned and made for the shore again.

A third craft, a cutter, which a number of passengers declared was actually flying the Italian flag, also made off in a hurry. I did not myself see the Italian flag.

The cement in the cargo settling into the hold apparently blocked the hole sufficiently to enable the powerful pumps to master the rush of water. The bulkhead between the flooded hold and the next section of the ship was cracked, but still holding.

Steaming very slowly so as not to increase the pressure on the bulkhead, the ship was off Port-Vendres within an hour and a half.

It was at first hoped that possibly with a British destroyer standing by she might still proceed to Marseilles in the morning. Within a few hours this hope and the bulkhead collapsed together.

Wind was rising and the sea beginning to be choppy. Distress rockets were again fired.

I went ashore in the ship's motor boat to explain the urgency of the danger to the port authorities, to hasten the sending of all possible aid. An hour or so later all the passengers had been hastily landed and the *Llandovery Castle* was on her way towards the beach.

It was pretty generally agreed that everything that could have been done by all those concerned was done, and done efficiently. The blame for the wrecking of the *Llandovery Castle* lies clearly on the shoulders of the British government which has so consistently failed to join with the democratic governments of Europe in putting an end to Fascist piracy on the high seas.

Daily Worker, 4 March 1937

MINERS TAKE KEY VILLAGE

Republicans Press Two Rebel Armies

North, where a howling gale off the Atlantic sent torrential rain lashing through the Asturian mountains, and south, on the blazing road between the sierra and the Mediterranean Sea, government troops passed two rebel armies in hard fighting yesterday.

Outside Oviedo, miners, forming the backbone of the attack, fought their way into the village of San Claudio, dominating, if not actually controlling, the only remaining road connecting the Oviedo garrison with rebel forces outside.

An Italian column, several thousand strong, which left Seville by road for the Oviedo front on the evening of 20 February, has not been heard of since. There is the possibility that it may be thrown into action within the next few hours.

On the broken front which, in widely separated sections, runs roughly from the Mediterranean coast at Adra, west of Almería, through the mountain valleys to a point north of Motril, government troops resisted heavy enemy attacks and in the coastal sector scored a small advance against grim enemy resistance.

Immediately west of Adra the coast road is relatively easy to defend, with advance by either side correspondingly difficult. The road is simply a ledge carved out of the side of mountains falling precipitously to the sea.

Just east of Adra, on the other hand, the ledge suddenly broadens out into an almost entirely flat coastal plain stretching almost to Almería itself.

Just outside Almería the mountains close in to the sea again, and the road runs close to the sea with very little space between it and the precipices on either side.

The vigour of the defence – and counter-attack – at Adra and in the mountains north of the main insurgent line east of Málaga, are a sufficient answer to those who thought that after the Italians marched into Málaga they would without difficulty roll up the front all the way to Almería and beyond.

The story of the bloody chaos and horror of the refugee women and children spattered by Fascist machine-gun fire on the Málaga-Almería road is already history.

The other side of it is the colossal achievement of the Republicans who, in the midst of all that, reorganised their forces and are still holding the road in front of Adra.

Only a few days ago I myself talked to men just arrived from Seville, who described the hurried departure from there of the Italian relief column for Oviedo and the panicky anxiety of the Seville command at the prospect of the loss of the city.

Oviedo is in three ways a key-point.

First, it contains the most important and best-equipped arms factory in Spain. For the first two months of the war at least I do not think there was a single rifle in use on the government side which had not been made in Oviedo.

Second, it dominates Asturias, and the possibility of any advance out of Asturias southwards over the mountain ranges depends on the possession of Oviedo.

Oviedo is the key to the mining valley which runs up beyond Mieres to the high passes south of there. An enemy could still make a stubborn resistance in the mountain passes even after the loss of Oviedo.

But without Oviedo, a large scale attack on the passes is itself an impossibility.

In other words, without holding Oviedo, any force in Asturias is condemned to a generally defensive position, its offensive action necessarily concentrated on the attack on the town itself.

Third, without Oviedo, the possibility of concerted advance from other points of the northern fronts, out of Santander and Biscay is at the best badly hampered since – for the reason given above – Asturias would be unable to cooperate in such an advance until Oviedo was taken, and the enemy in Oviedo would present a perpetual threat to the right flank; a threat, that is to say, offered by an enemy holding a strong position already north of the largest east-west running mountain barrier.

Daily Worker, 9 March 1937

REBELS ADMIT AID FROM ITALY

Interview By Franco

While the British capitalist press and the British government maintain a dead silence on the size and character of the Italian invasion and occupation of Spain – now amounting to 200,000 – General Franco himself has given the show away in a sensational, authorised interview with a French Fascist newspaper.

The paper is *Gringoire*. The interviewer is Raymond Recouly, who, almost since the outbreak of the war, has at intervals acted as a mouthpiece for the Fascist forces.

The sum total of the interview is an open declaration by General Franco that he has had an enormous increase in men and materials, so great as entirely to alter the strategic situation in Spain, and a statement by Recouly that Italians are those who have made this change possible.

To understand why this extraordinary indiscretion should have been permitted by the General and the French Fascist paper it is necessary to know the purpose of the interview.

Its purpose, as Recouly frankly admits at the end of the article, is to persuade the French reactionaries and as many of the French Centre as possible that Franco is now certain of victory, and thus simultaneously to spread alarm and defeatism among the democrats and to rally forces for an attempt to upset the Blum government by a Fascist coup, followed by open support for Fascist policy in Spain.

This explains why General Franco has committed the indiscretion of stating that he has now received forces sufficient to alter the whole military situation.

Recouly asked him why he had so far failed to win the war. He replied in part as follows:

'Certain military critics have reproached me with making a frontal attack upon Madrid instead of encircling it. But how could I at that time have succeeded in such an encirclement? I was without the men and the materials, which today I have abundantly at my disposal. What I could not do then I can do now. I can do it when I want to and as I want to.'

Following this frank admission of the arrival of new forces Recouly underlined the part played by Italy, concluding with the significant words:

'The experience of Abyssinia proves the situation. Mussolini is not a man to use small means.'

It is interesting to note that the cautious *Manchester Guardian* today raises the figure of the interventionist troops in Spain from 80,000, the highest previously given, except in the *Daily Worker* reports, to a minimum of 100,000.

Daily Worker, 15 March 1937

MADRID ROUTS ITALIANS

'A day of glory for the Republican troops' was the description of the Madrid Defence Committee of the rout of two mechanised divisions of regular Italian troops, some 30,000 men, on the Guadalajara front on Saturday.

It was the fourth day of Franco's big drive on Madrid. As the Italian regulars advanced, government airmen, defying the terrible flying conditions, swooped down from the low-lying clouds and raked the advancing troops with bombs and machine-gun fire.

Simultaneously ten battalions of the International Brigade launched a frontal attack with cold steel.

The morale of the Italian conscripts broke. Whole battalions turned and fled in disorder, leaving their arms behind them.

Tanks, artillery, munitions and guns fell into the hands of the government forces. The spirit of men fighting for democracy proved greater than the spirit of the Italian conscripts.

The government registered that day its greatest victory over the Fascist invaders.

At the same time as this victory comes the revelation of the vast extent of Fascist intervention.

Yesterday part of that invading army was licking its wounds and trying to hold off the pressure of the advance by the victorious Spanish People's Army.

Even the boastful Fascists of Burgos, always clamorous in their shouts of victory, admit that their advance has been stopped.

From the cold facts and figures of official communiqués emerges an epic story of men fighting for freedom against the Fascist invaders.

After four days of fierce fighting, Franco launched his biggest push.

30,000 Italian regulars, with artillery, tanks, machine-guns and all the other equipment of modern war, were marching to the attack down the narrow Tajuna Valley.

Weather was bad. Attack from the air seemed impossible. Then from the low clouds came thirty government aeroplanes, their pilots defying what seemed almost certain death.

Low over the Italian troops they swooped, machine-guns in action, dropping bombs as they swept over the marching columns.

Eight times they flew over the attacking forces, dropping nearly 500 bombs, firing 200,000 rounds of machine-gun ammunition.

The Italians broke and fled before this hail of death and before the charge of ten battalions of working-class fighters in the International Brigade.

The extent of the rout can be seen from the report of the Madrid Defence Committee:

'Trijueque (forty-five miles from Madrid) has fallen into our hands and we have captured magnificent war booty, including twelve pieces of artillery, two lorry-loads of munitions, sixty machine-guns, anti-aircraft guns, two lorry loads of food, a field kitchen and prisoners.'

Then, in a communique from the Air Ministry:

'The commander of the air squadron is of the impression that one of the Italian divisions was destroyed.

'Our aviators clearly saw entire battalions in disorderly and precipitate retreat.

'The aeroplanes followed, machine-gunning the fugitives and causing them great losses.

'Bombs caused great damage to the war material of the Italians. Tanks and lorries were wrecked and set on fire.'

Altogether some twenty-three tanks were put out of action by planes and dynamiters.

The attack on this side of Madrid is definitely broken. From other fronts the government also reports successes.

On the Córdoba front the advance has been pushed to Villa Nueva, west of Caso Blanco, government troops have reached within two kilometres of the village despite the heavy rains.

On the Jaén front rebel guards trapped in the Sanctuary of Santa María de la Cabeza, north of Andújar, are claimed to be very short of food, which is dropped to them from rebel aeroplanes.

The machines have not been able to fly over for the last few days and the guards were obliged to make a sortie to try and capture loyal food convoys. Their attack made at dawn is said to have been successfully repulsed.

On the Aragon front there has been a fierce artillery duel between the government batteries at Puerto de Santa Eloisa and the insurgent guns in the Pyrenees sector.

Rain is holding up operations, and the rest of the front is quiet.

Three rebel planes bombed the Sabadell, Badalona, Gramanet, San Adrian and Barriada Artigas districts on the outskirts of Barcelona yesterday, their objectives being an aerodrome, an electric plant and a factory. Eighty bombs were dropped, but little damage was done, and two persons were killed and six wounded.

Daily Worker, 16 March 1937

REBEL MADRID DRIVE COMPLETE FAILURE BUT POSITION IS STILL DANGEROUS

MADRID, Monday.

Madrid is still free from the threat of isolation. The Guadalajara attack by regular divisions of Italian troops has been definitely halted.

The front is temporarily stabilised at a point west of Trijueque and the Madrid-Saragossa highway, and on a line south-east, but the entire rebel line is still far from the Guadalajara-Cuenca road, and therefore unrelated to the Fascist position in the neighbourhood of Arganda.

As the Italian offensive aimed to bring the rebel lines west, across the Valencia road, completing the Fascist communications from Saragossa to Seville, the fifth and greatest attack against Madrid may be pronounced a complete failure.

In fact, the government has now taken the initiative on this front, conducting counter-attacks, which yesterday alone netted over 100 Italian prisoners, and the twenty-odd machine-guns with which they were defending a huge country mansion.

Despite these encouraging facts, the Madrid situation, viewed from this front, may be described as very serious. The threat of a great drive by a heavily armed Italian army, capable of completely encircling Madrid, persists.

The government initiative is a counter-attack and not a counter-offensive. The loyalist pushes involve relatively few men and great distances, as has been the case in all government offensive pushes so far.

In the opinion of authoritative observers, the Fascists have not yet put into play the full force of the Italian reserves available for use on this front.

Militarily, the situation is grave, but political factors balance the scale. Prisoners reveal that the 'successful' Italian troops have no fighting morale and are particularly unwilling to fight against their fellow Italians.

Chapter Four

COCKBURN'S PASSPORT, THE POUM RISING, ALMERÍA

*After retrieving his passport from the Foreign Office, Cockburn
returned to Spain in April 1937 and covered the fighting on the
Madrid front and the fall of Bilbao. He reported on the POUM rising
in Barcelona and then travelled south to cover the situation in Almería
after the Nazi naval bombardment. The tone of his despatches reflects
the increasingly bitter divisions which were appearing within the
Republican-controlled areas, and within the Left internationally.*

Daily Worker, 24 March 1937

FOREIGN OFFICE BANS PITCAIRN

Effort to Gag 'Daily Worker' On Spain

The British government has given formal orders to the Passport
Office to refuse Frank Pitcairn, *Daily Worker* reporter in Spain,
a permit to return to his work in Madrid and has instructed the
Passport Office to stamp his passport with the words 'Not valid
for Spain'.

The raw facts are that the government and its Foreign Office
have by this action –

committed an open discriminatory attack upon the *Daily
Worker* and its news service;

undertaken an attack of an unprecedented kind on the
existing liberties of British newspapers;

and declared themselves publicly as enemies of fair reporting
from the government side in Spain.

The affair has already created first astonishment and then
indignation among those British newspapermen of all parties

who are jealous for the remaining liberties of their profession and of the press.

MPs recognised the far-reaching character of the attack upon the freedom of newspaper reporting, and its significance as an illumination of the policy of the government equally at home and internationally.

Questions are being asked in the House of Commons this afternoon.

Almost at the same moment when the Passport Office and Foreign Office were forbidding Frank Pitcairn to return to Spain as a reporter for this newspaper, they were giving out permits to other journalists to go to Spain.

At one stage of the proceedings a subordinate official at the Foreign Office informed Pitcairn that the Foreign Office proposed not merely to render his passport invalid for Spain, but to seize the passport altogether.

Less than twenty-four hours after this announcement had been made at the Foreign Office, the passport – invalidated for Spain – was returned without explanation by the Passport Office.

The position is that under the provisions of the Non-Intervention Agreement and the regulations for the prevention of volunteers going to Spain to assist in fighting the Italian troops which continue to pour into rebel territory, it is necessary to get from the British Foreign Office an 'endorsement' on one's passport before proceeding to Spain.

The endorsement is supposed to be given to anyone proceeding to Spain on 'legitimate' business – that is to say business not prohibited by the terms of the Non-Intervention Agreement.

On the strength of this endorsement on the passport of a British subject the French authorities are enabled to give permission to cross the French frontier to Spain. Without this endorsement the French authorities are compelled by the iniquitous Non-Intervention Agreement to stop travellers at the frontier.

Daily Worker, 29 March 1937

TORIES WORRIED ABOUT FRANK PITCAIRN

(From Our Parliamentary Correspondent)

HOUSE OF COMMONS, Wednesday. Certain Tory MPs seem to be uncommonly interested in the activities of Claud Cockburn, Special Correspondent of the *Daily Worker* in Spain (who writes under the pen name of Frank Pitcairn).

Mr Denville (Con., Newcastle-on-Tyne, C.), who has already raised the question before, asked the Foreign Secretary in the House of Commons today if he was now in a position to inform the House regarding the activities of Mr Cockburn, a British subject, 'who is acting as assistant publicity agent for the Madrid government'.

Mr Eden replied that so far as he could ascertain, Mr Cockburn had been engaged on press and propaganda work on behalf of the Spanish government.

Mr Denville: Is it not a fact that this man, in co-operation with another man who is a Communist leader, is running the whole of the Red publicity which comes into this country?

Mr Gallacher (Com., West Fife): Is the Foreign Secretary aware that Mr Cockburn is correspondent of a good newspaper, and is a better publicity agent than the Marquis del Moral?* (Laughter.)

Neither question was answered.

Claud Cockburn – The Facts

The facts about Claud Cockburn are as follows:

Last July, following the Fascist rebellion in Spain, he was sent by the *Daily Worker* as special correspondent, first to Barcelona and then to Madrid.

His reports, under the pen-name of Frank Pitcairn, attracted immediate attention, and he became world-famous as one of the

* The Marquis del Moral was a leading pro-Franco propagandist in London.

best correspondents in Spain.

Following his return for a brief spell to this country, just before Easter, the Foreign Office made an effort to prevent his resumption of his work in Spain, by refusing to furnish him with a passport endorsement, which, they pretended, was necessary to enable him to enter Spain.

Immediate and indignant protest was expressed by many prominent journalists and public persons, as well as the National Union of Journalists, of which Mr Cockburn is a member.

Despite the obstruction of the Foreign Office, Mr Cockburn, again on the instructions of the *Daily Worker* Editorial Board, returned to Spain, where he was admitted by the government, and continued his work as correspondent.

Mr Cockburn is a member of the *Daily Worker* editorial staff, and his work in Spain is conducted under the control of the Editorial Board which sent him there. – EDITORIAL BOARD.

Daily Worker, 9 April 1937

FRANK PITCAIRN IN MADRID NOW

Return Is In Defence Of British Civil Rights

Frank Pitcairn, Daily Worker *special correspondent in Spain, is again in Madrid. Below is printed a message telephoned by Pitcairn from Spain immediately on his return.*

This is not merely the return of a foreign correspondent to his work, but the assertion by the Daily Worker *and by Frank Pitcairn of the freedom of the press, of the right of newspapermen to carry on their work unhindered by government opposition, and of the liberty of a British citizen to travel freely abroad.*

Readers of the Daily Worker *will remember that when Pitcairn wished to return to Spain after visiting this country the*

Foreign Office refused to give his passport the endorsement
which it considered necessary. That refusal aroused a chorus of
protest from every defender of democratic rights and civil
liberties in the country.

Pitcairn's passport received no endorsement. This, however,
represented no legal right on the government's part to prevent
Pitcairn from going to Madrid, where he now is. The Daily
Worker *will continue, as in the past, to receive messages which*
tell the truth about the Fascist attack on Spain, despatches that
are demanded by all lovers of democracy, messages which tell
the full story of a people's fight for liberty.

MADRID, Thursday.

The lull on the Madrid front has been almost unbroken, except
for small local actions for three days.

This pause in the actual fighting emphasises the immense
activity behind the line. It is just five months since the defence of
Madrid began, and I can without exaggeration say that the
present development of the army is a quite decisive result of the
work done during November in the organisation of forces
capable of holding the city against the first Fascist attack.

Then it was a question of turning existing military groups into
a disciplined defence force. Today it is a question of organising
the vast available resources on the government side into a
striking force capable of finally turning the tables on the enemy.

One of the most important results of the great government
victory at Guadalajara has been the immense impetus given to
the development of the new armies; for the victory, apart from
everything else, proved that the work done since November
(particularly the Spanish Communist Party's manifesto, which
called for the creation of the regular People's Army) was along
the right lines.

The advance of the government troops in the south during the
whole of the last eight days is having a similar effect.

In the newspaper *Politica* this morning was a frank and
interesting leader drawing comparisons between the situation on
the Córdoba front as it was before the forces were reorganised
on a regular army basis, and the situation today.

Politica points the moral of the situation, and states that now
is the moment to accelerate the final victory of the government
forces by speeding-up the process of militarisation.

Among the things the responsible newspapers are demanding are the creation of very large forces of properly-trained reserves, an immediate speed-up in the developments of war industry, and the acceptance of the regular army system through the whole of Spain – meaning, of course, principally, Catalonia.

The United Syndicalist Army of Catalonia today publishes from the UGT a strongly worded manifesto making firm demands and calling for action to bring Catalonia at long last to the military level of the rest of anti-fascist Spain.

The *Fighter's Voice*, organ of the People's Army, also puts forth the demand for a still greater acceleration of the process of mobilisation, for, despite a series of defeats, international Fascism will make new, desperate efforts against Spain.

'The enemy is making preparations, and it is our duty to anticipate his plans as well as wreck them.'

In view of the latest news of the fresh troop landings at Cadiz, this might well be addressed to the democrats of England, whose part in the struggle for Spanish independence and European democracy becomes daily more important.

Daily Worker, 12 April 1937

FIERCE NEW MADRID BATTLE

Republicans Drive On As Rebels Shell City With Heavy Guns

MADRID, Sunday.

In windy weather, with gusts of rain and low, driving clouds, which badly hampered aviation, the Republican attack in the Casa de Campo continued this afternoon and is still going on on both fronts.

Earlier in the day the Fascists sent seventeen or eighteen shells into Madrid's crowded Sunday streets. It was the most intensive bombardment the civilian population have been made to suffer since the very first days of this year.

Whereas in the past the shelling of the city has usually been carried out from one gun, firing at long intervals, they were sending them over this morning from at least three guns at once.

I saw three wounded women with the blood streaming over their Sunday-best clothes, being carried into the hospital in the middle of the morning. They had been hit by flying splinters while strolling in one of the central squares.

The number of civilians dead and wounded is considerable. The military result is, of course, nil, as usual in these outbursts of Fascist spite against the city they cannot take.

Out at the front the Republican attack started over on the right flank in the neighbourhood of Aravaca and Partridge Hill, soon after two o'clock.

I have passed the whole of the far side of Partridge Hill, which is wooded half-way up and quite bare on top, like a bald-headed man with a fringe of thick hair. It was thick with the brownish-white smoke of the bursting shells.

Then came the machine-guns, and for a quarter of an hour there was a roar of battle along the whole of the sector of the front.

From Partridge Hill the ground rises in lesser levels and undulations to the slopes of Garabitas Hill, the very centre of the Fascist position in the Casa de Campo.

Then the ground levels out somewhat, stretching in a partially wooded slope – sloping up away from Madrid – as high as the Extramadura Road, the southern edge of Casa de Campo.

A short distance behind the lake in the Casa de Campo, the lake being now behind the government lines, are a number of houses strongly fortified and held as machine-gun posts by the Fascists.

For more than four months – ever since they realised that they were not going to walk into Madrid – the enemy has been fortifying the position in the Casa de Campo. The trenches, pill-boxes and concrete defence works on Garabitas Hill are probably as strong as the defence works in many divisions of the Western Front during the Great War.

This is the first time during this war that attacks have been carried out against such positions – positions in which an advance of even a few hundred yards can be counted a good day's work.

A few minutes after the machine-gun fire on the right flank reached its peak of intensity the shelling began on the left bank and machine-gun fire broke out from government positions there.

Among the enemy soldiers to be seen hurrying about behind their lines a number of Moors, in their African capes, were clearly visible.

Of the artillery bombardment the left or southern bit of the Government pincer was once again being worked into action.

At the same time with the advance already made on Friday and Saturday on the right, the position of the rebel forces in University City has become extremely grave, though there seems to be a good deal of doubt as to how far they can be totally cut off from all supplies until a considerable advance and consolidation of the government positions has been made.

The panorama of the front this afternoon and yesterday, with the magnificent fleet of the government bombers yesterday dropping a huge weight of bombs in packet after packet from end to end of the line, the guns making really excellent shooting against the defences of Garabitas Hill, and the houses beyond the lake, the tanks rolling into action at point after point, and the machine-guns coming into place as the infantry struggles forward at the two extremities of the line, was a thrilling picture of the new power and efficiency of the disciplined organisation and material power of the new Republican Army.

Daily Worker, 19 April 1937

GALLACHER IN MADRID'S TRENCHES

Duchess And Party Under Fire

MADRID, Sunday.

William Gallacher, Communist MP lived through some of the most vivid hours of all his life of struggle yesterday and today, when he visited comrades in the front-line trenches on the central front.

The news that Gallacher was in the trenches roused scenes of enthusiasm like those seen when Pollitt visited the comrades. It is easy enough to describe how the men of that battalion greeted Gallacher, how they cheered and how they sang the International. What is not so easy to describe or to make real to you who are reading this a long way off is just what that enthusiasm, that cheering and that singing means when it is done by men who have endured what these men have endured in their struggle for the independence of Spain and the freedom of Europe.

I cannot tell you in detail the story of these men's struggle during the past week, because that would amount to giving information to the enemy.

I can only tell you that among all those who have fought here side by side with their Spanish comrades during the battles and the long, wearisome vigils of the past seventy days, there are none who have surpassed the heroism of the men who yesterday and today greeted Gallacher with a spirit which even he had no words to describe.

I suppose Gallacher has seen in his life as many examples of heroism as any living man. He told me that in all his life he had never seen anything to surpass what he saw in those trenches on his visit there yesterday.

It was an interesting and significant scene this morning, when Gallacher met at breakfast with the members of the Women's Parliamentary Delegation – the Duchess of Atholl, Eleanor Rathbone, Dame Rachel Crowdy and Ellen Wilkinson – and exchanged experiences and impressions.

The Duchess of Atholl had plenty to say about the iniquity of the shelling of Madrid, which reached its all-time record yesterday with a casualty list among civilians of 110.

One shell sent the plaster flying from the ceiling of the restaurant where the delegation was at lunch, and when they left men were still mopping up the blood spilt in the doorway by three men and a woman who had been standing there a few minutes before.

Just across the street a militia-guard on duty outside the theatre had his legs hacked off by huge pieces of broken glass, driven like enormous razors, by the force of the explosion.

A little further down the road I saw the brains of a woman plastered against a wall, while her legs lay in a pool of blood in the gutter.

The enemy were apparently firing with two batteries at once.

I counted six shells whistling by in something less than fifteen seconds. A British comrade with considerable experience of artillery, who had helped to carry some wounded outside the café where he was sitting, told me the shells were cordite shells of the type known by artillery men as 'Demoralisation Shells'. The point about them is that the charge of cordite in them bursts them into fragments, even smaller than ordinary shrapnel, reducing next to nothing their capacity for penetration into any military defensive, and raising to maximum their destructive effect on human life when they burst in an open street.

The pretence that they are firing at a military objective was finally blown to pieces yesterday by the rebels themselves, when they broadcast their shells all over the city, simultaneously tearing to pieces people standing in queues, people simply going from one office to another, people riding in the tramcars.

Daily Worker, 29 April 1937

BIG OFFENSIVE TO SAVE BILBAO

MADRID, Wednesday.

A national effort, an offensive on all fronts to relieve pressure on the Bilbao front, is the slogan raised throughout the Madrid streets today.

The position on the Bilbao front is very grave. According, however, to expert information direct from that front which I have received here today, it is not by any means desperate.

A united effort by government forces operating on other fronts can save it by giving time for the new Basque army to get itself organised efficiently, as the army of the central front is already organised.

Three weeks ago, at the time of the last big rebel drive led by the Germans against Bilbao, there was actually no Basque army in existence. Then came the great attack in the Casa del Campo, which was Madrid's gift to Bilbao.

The result was an almost immediate slackening of the rebel attack in the Basque country. When a particularly heavy enemy barrage of shell-fire opened in the Casa del Campo on the third of those days the soldiers in our lines raised a cheer, shouting,

'The guns have come from Bilbao.'

The delay was intended to be used and was used for the organisation of a regular army out of the innumerable militia groups operating more or less disjointedly under the orders of the Basque government.

Today saw the first fruits of the delay which Madrid won for Bilbao.

There is published this morning the decree predicting a new regular army of the Basque country along the organisational lines first proposed by the Communist Party for the Army of the Centre in the early autumn.

The basis of the new Basque Army is, of course, formed by the existing militia battalions which, however, now merge their semi- independence in the brigades and divisions of a single unified regular military force, exactly as happened on the central front in the early winter of last year.

At the same time, although they are in favour of taking part in fortification work, they are by the same decree mobilised for the purpose.

Ahora this morning, in a leading article headed 'Let us Save Basque Country', points out that this time the offensive has got to be something more than an offensive by Madrid alone. There has got to be an offensive on all fronts. There has got to be a co-ordinated plan of general offensive and to launch an offensive successfully there has to be a well-centralised command directing all operations.

Daily Worker, 11 May 1937

PITCAIRN LIFTS BARCELONA VEIL

Trotskyist Rising As Signal

VALENCIA, Monday.
This will turn out to have been fateful days in the history of Spain. It is one of the most critical moments of the war. The Germans and Italians are at the gates of Bilbao. Catalonia is full of German and Italian agents working desperately to reorganise

the rebellion against the People's Front government, which was crushed last week by the forces of the People's Army, co-operating with the people of Catalonia.

Today, the people of Spain are discussing one thing: the message of the Communist Party radioed from a Valencia meeting of the Party to every town and village in the country on Sunday morning.

That meeting will mark a stage in the struggle in Spain for freedom as important and decisive as the meeting of the Communist Party in the Monumental Cinema in Madrid in the summer of 1935, when the Communist Party announced their proposals for the People's Front; as important as the manifesto issued in December, 1936, when the Communist Party called for the final constitution of the regular army and of the people and the introduction of compulsory service.

These actions of the Communist Party changed the course of the history of Spain. Yesterday's meeting was in the same category.

Thousands of loudspeakers, set up in every public place in the towns and villages of Republican Spain, in the trenches all along the battle-front of the Republic, brought the message of the Communist Party at this fateful hour, straight to the soldiers and the struggling people of this hard-pressed hard-fighting Republic.

The speakers were Valdés, former Councillor of Public Works in the Catalan government, Uribe, Minister of Agriculture in the government of Spain, Díaz, Secretary of the Communist Party of Spain, Pasionaria, and Hernández, Minister of Education.

Then, as now, in the forefront of everything stand the Fascist menace to Bilbao and Catalonia.

There is a specially dangerous feature about the situation in Catalonia. We know now that the German and Italian agents, who poured into Barcelona ostensibly in order to 'prepare' the notorious 'Congress of the Fourth International', had one big task. It was this:

They were – in co-operation with the local Trotskyists – to prepare a situation of disorder and bloodshed, in which it would be possible for the Germans and Italians to declare that they were 'unable to exercise naval control on the Catalan coasts effective-ly', because of 'the disorder prevailing in Barcelona', and were, therefore, 'unable to do otherwise' than land forces in Barcelona.

In other words, what was being prepared was a situation in which the Italian and German governments could land troops or marines quite openly on the Catalan coasts, declaring that they were doing so 'in order to preserve order'.

That was the aim. Probably that is still the aim. The instrument for all this lay ready to hand for the Germans and Italians in the shape of the Trotskyist organisation known as the POUM.

The POUM, acting in co-operation with well-known criminal elements, and with certain other deluded persons in the anarchist organisations, planned, organised and led the attack in the rearguard, accurately timed to coincide with the attack on the front at Bilbao.

In the past, the leaders of the POUM have frequently sought to deny their complicity as agents of a Fascist cause against the People's Front. This time they are convicted out of their own mouths as clearly as their allies, operating in the Soviet Union, who confessed to the crimes of espionage, sabotage, and attempted murder against the government of the Soviet Union.

Copies of *La Batalla*, issued on and after 2 May, and the leaflets issued by the POUM before and during the killings in Barcelona, set down the position in cold print.

In the plainest terms the POUM declares it is the enemy of the People's Government. In the plainest terms it calls upon its followers to turn their arms in the same direction as the Fascists, namely, against the government of the People's Front and the anti-fascist fighters.

900 dead and 2,500 wounded is the figure officially given by Díaz as the total in terms of human slaughter of the POUM attack in Barcelona.

It was not, by any means, Díaz pointed out, the first of such attacks. Why was it, for instance, that at the moment of the big Italian drive at Guadalajara, the Trotskyists and their deluded anarchist friends attempted a similar rising in another district? Why was it that the same thing happened two months before at the time of the heavy Fascist attack at Jarama, when, while Spaniards and Englishmen, and honest anti-fascists of every nation in Europe, were being killed holding Arganda Bridge, the Trotskyist swine suddenly produced their arms 200 kilometres from the front, and attacked in the rear?

Daily Worker, 17 May 1937

REPUBLIC ROUNDS UP HIDDEN ARMS

BARCELONA, Sunday.

Tomorrow the anti-fascist forces of the Republic will start rounding up all those scores of concealed weapons which ought to be at the front and are not.

The decree ordering this action affects the whole of the Republic. It is, however, in Catalonia that its effects are likely to be the most interesting and important.

With it, the struggle to 'put Catalonia on a war footing', which has been going on for months and was resisted with open violence by the POUM and its friends in the first week of May, enters a new phase.

This weekend may well be a turning-point. If the decree is successfully carried out it means:

First: That the groups led by the POUM who rose against the government last week will lose their main source of strength, namely, their arms.

Second: That, as a result of this, their ability to hamper by terrorism the efforts of the anti-fascist workers to get the war factories on to a satisfactory basis will be sharply reduced.

Third: That the arms at present hidden will be available for use on the front, where they are badly needed.

Fourth: That in future those who steal arms from the front or steal arms in transit to the front will be liable to immediate arrest and trial as ally of the fascist enemy.

Included in the weapons which have to be turned in are rifles, carbines, machine-guns, machine-pistols, trench mortars, field guns, armoured cars, hand-grenades, and all other sorts of bombs.

The list gives you an idea of the sort of armaments accumulated by the Fascist conspirators and brought into the open for the first time last week.

There were actually all sorts of arms used by them in the outrage. There were the arms which they have been stealing for months past, and hidden, and there were arms such as tanks, which they stole from the barracks just at the beginning of the rising.

It is clear that scores of machine-guns and several thousand rifles are still in their possession. It does not need much imagination to figure out what these weapons could effect on the Aragon front at the moment of the Fascist menace at Bilbao, nor, contrariwise, what their loss will mean to the allies of Fascism who create trouble in the rearguard.

It is the size and character of the armaments they have accumulated, rather than the number of men involved in the attack which counts for the heavy loss of life in Barcelona during the fighting.

It accounts for the fact that they were able to create violent disorder without, as a matter of fact, any mass support worth speaking of – that and the fact that the government was extraordinarily and, as some think, excessively anxious to avoid drastic action until drastic action was forced upon them.

The events in Tarragona are a sufficient sample of the character of the movement. In that town the rebels had a tank and several machine-guns, not to mention hand-grenades, rifles, etc., yet exactly thirty-two anti-fascist air force mechanics were sufficient to arrest and disarm the lot of them inside of a couple of hours.

The POUM itself, in a resolution just issued by its Central Committee, admits that the whole thing was futile and had no prospect of success. With this it explains its 'strategic retreat'.

Las Noticias, organ of the UGT of Catalonia, commenting on this resolution, says:

'The leading elements of the POUM, who, during the tragic days of the struggle, were issuing leaflets and manifestoes inciting to revolution, and backing up the groups which had risen against the legally constituted government of the Generalidad, and who recommended all these groups and their own members to keep their arms, have had to confess that it was a movement without any revolutionary objective, and without direction.

'The Trotskyist agent-provocateurs took part in the rising and now publicly state that the affair was a putsch.

'Provocation and cynicism. How long is it going to be possible that at such delicate moments as these the *agents-provocateurs* are to be allowed to work at liberty? The leaders of the POUM, together with the so-called Friends of Durruti, have publicly declared themselves active participants in the subversive movement.

'The members of both organisations have been described as they deserve to be by the really revolutionary working masses and by the anti-fascists in general. Their own leaders – workers conscious of their responsibility as members of an organisation which they believe to be Marxist, and the responsible leaders of the CNT – have publicly repudiated the POUM and Friends of Durruti.'

Noticias then refers to an agreement reached as a result of which all members of the Central Committee of the POUM will be expelled from the union branches of the UGT, together with all others who sided with the rebels last week, to a similar agreement by the CNT to expel those of its members proved to have taken part in the rising.

'These measures of public safety together with the action of the courts in punishing the guilty, will be our rearguard in a position to undertake effective action in the war and will permit Catalonia to produce, in a very short space of time, an army corps which our comrades in Aragon, the Basque country and the central front need so badly.'

The belief that if drastic action against the saboteurs and armed enemies in the rearguard can be quickly carried out, the Eastern Army may soon be turning into a formidable fighting force is not, I think, over optimistic.

The fact is – and it is of capital importance – that in the weeks before the 3 May rising the unification and militarisation of the Aragon Army had already begun.

Despite the frantic efforts of the POUM to stop it, the first steps corresponding roughly to those taken in Madrid in November had already been taken towards the development of an army out of the trade union and political parties' militia.

In some cases the change existed only on paper. That is to say, the same organisations were simply renamed without being really organised on a regular army basis. But it is of the utmost importance to notice, and to remember, that among the men of the Aragon front, themselves, and among the new recruits who went up there, the process of unification was going ahead very fast, so that already before the May rising, it was true to say that very large sections of the Aragon army could no longer be classed as purely anarchist, or purely United Socialist units.

While retaining their original names many of them were in

fact composed of elements of all parties and organisations, just
as was the old Fifth Regiment on the central front. There were,
for instance, a very large percentage of fine anarchist fighters
fighting in the ranks of the Karl Marx Division originally
organised by the United Socialist Party and large numbers of the
United Socialist Party fighting in the ranks of the anarchist
battalions.

Following the appointment of General Pozas and the
constitution of the Eastern Army, this more or less spontaneous
process has received official impetus and will follow the lines of
the creation of the regular army first on the central front then in
the south, and most recently in the Basque country.

There is no doubt that the spontaneous unification and
militarisation of the army already in progress in April was one
of the many features which decided the POUM and its friends to
make the attack in Barcelona that they did.

It was characteristic that their friends directed many of their
most violent attacks openly against the formation of a regular
army. For the experiences of Madrid and of the southern front
where this reorganisation turned defeat into victory almost
overnight had shown that the absence of such a force has been
on each front the Fascists' best hope.

There is perhaps no phase of their activity in which the
Poumsters have more notably shown themselves up for what
they are than in this long-drawn campaign designed to prevent
the formation of a regular army, like that of the Centre on the
Aragon front.

Yet it is important to note that the effect of their campaign
was so small among the masses that when the government
mobilisation decree was issued in February, more than eighty
per cent of the men of Catalonia who were liable to be called up
under the decree, rushed to present themselves voluntarily even
before the orders were received, proving that whatever fault
there may have been in the organisation of Catalonia for war,
the will of the Catalan people is as clear and strong in favour of
organised battle against the Fascists as it was with the people of
Madrid.

Daily Worker, 3 June 1937

DOGS HOWL IN EMPTY ALMERÍA, PEOPLE HIDE IN CAVES

VALENCIA, Wednesday.
Last night I stood at a window in Almería and listened. Absolute silence except for first one and then another dog. The dogs ran about the streets looking for food.

Madrid and Valencia are silent at night, but that is a different sort of silence. By an incident of small magnitude you are aware of hundreds of thousands of people all around you, you can hear them breathing. Almería at night is dead. 65,000 people lived there before the war. Tonight there are not many more than 1,000 in the whole city. The Nazis have driven them out.

Above the city you can see the ancient Roman ruins, and you begin to understand what the Romans felt like when the barbarians came.

Supposing this were Southampton or Dover. Most of the population wandering about in the New Forest or the Downs, looking for a comfortable cave to settle down in; thousands of others coming into town every morning early and leaving again at night – for fear the Nazis should come again.

There is still a certain amount of work for civilians to do in Almería. For instance, the first man I saw at work in the morning was the coffin-maker, who is busy already and expects to be busier still. Is this, you wonder, really the state of things to come?

The big construction works in the city is something that looks as though it were going to be an underground railway. It turned out to be a vast system of subterranean bomb-proof refuges and passages for the civilians from the Germans when they next put the principles of totalitarian war into practice.

During the daytime you can in many parts of the town have the illusion that nothing at all has happened. You would expect to see something tremendously spectacular. On the contrary, things look what we have taken to calling 'normal'.

For instance, there is the facade of the Hotel Simon. It looks all right. Nothing has happened there you think. Then you step inside and find that one quarter of the roof has been shattered by a German shell and the rest of the roof is falling down at intervals in small showers of tile and plaster.

Over there is the civilian hospital. It appears untouched. You go upstairs and find that where the back ward was there is literally nothing left.

There were no sick people there for the reason that at one o'clock in the morning there was an air-raid alarm signal and, the Germans being the way they are about hospitals, the invalids were brought downstairs.

They lay in the passageway some two hours later listening to the shells go whistling methodically into this quarter and the rest of the city.

The shells fired systematically, directed by the German Admiral, reached that street. One shell blew the back of the hospital to bits. The next ripped open the roof of San Sebastián church, the third, scheduled by the Nazis for that section of the city, hit the street just beyond.

Two burst in the air above the street, spraying shrapnel on to the houses within reach. They also fired shrapnel shells into the other streets. This was a good idea of the Germans since people who ran out from the houses had a good chance of being killed by shrapnel in the open streets.

I met a young doctor, a very normal person, looking like an average young doctor of a large provincial town. His name is Lewis Criada. What happened to the Criada family is typical of what happened to people in Almería when the Nazis ran up the battleflag.

Lewis Criada himself was working at the military hospital. A shell fell in the garden. All over the town great puffs of smoke and thick clouds of red brick dust began to come up until they hung over the place like a cloud.

The ambulance men driving through the fire of shells began dashing up with wounded. Then when they started to operate they found the water, electricity and gas had all been cut off by the shelling.

Meantime, Criada's old mother and father had been asleep in their bedroom on the second floor of a block of little flats on rising ground just behind the centre of the town.

The shutters were closed. They were awakened in the darkness by the whistling of the shells and the crashing all around. They dared not open the shutters to see what was happening.

Like thousands of other families in Almería that morning they cowered together in a corner of the room imagining, as people do in such a situation, that the corner would somehow be safer than anywhere else. They clung to one another for protection.

Then a shell exploded on the third floor and then they blew up the whole top of the house and buried the old couple down below in masses of plaster and broken glass.

Five seconds later a shell fell in Criada's own bedroom, fortunately empty, because he was working at the hospital.

Finally, at almost the same moment, the house in which Criada's sister lived across the street, Majadores Street, had its roof and part of its back wall smashed by another shell.

Just one family and all in less than an hour.

And the town, as I said, looked almost normal.

All along the main streets houses are pitted with shrapnel holes. Shells had exploded in the middle of the street making it as wide as Oxford Street – shrapnel holes two and three inches thick in the walls. They blew scores of holes through the iron shutters of shops. Nobody who was in that street when the Germans started up had any chance of escaping unmaimed.

When there is an air raid there usually come warnings. On this occasion the German fleet took care there should be no warning.

If the people in Almería had not been fooled so often they might believe that now at last the democratic powers are going to act to keep them safe from the German guns. They do not believe it. They believe that the People's Army and the magnificent Navy and Air Force of the Republic are already upon the road to final victory and peaceful Spain.

In the meantime, they do what their Roman forefathers did when they, too, were in danger of being attacked by wild beasts. They leave the city at night and go to the hills and live in caves in the rocks.

In the hotel where I stayed only three people had remained for the night. The waitresses had gone to the hills at five in the afternoon. Before they went they put in a dozen of the rooms a few scraps of meat and cold fish in case soldiers or other travellers on business should turn up and have to spend the night.

We ate one of these meals by candlelight and listened to the dogs howling in the empty street. This is Europe in 1937 …

Daily Worker, 22 June 1937

BILBAO ... WHAT NOW?

Bilbao has fallen. Its fall is a disaster.

There are those abroad who state that it is a decisive disaster. The whole Fascist propaganda machine is being turned on to try to prove that the fate of the war is now decided. That is the silliest sort of nonsense.

You can travel far and wide through Republican Spain without ever finding any informed person to believe that. Better still, you can look at the hard facts and the cold figures of the situation – military, economic and financial – of Republican Spain today, and see that despite their victory at Bilbao, the Germans and Italians and all those who support them, are the victims of a terrible illusion if they think that they are on the way to winning the war.

They are not. Even at the very moment of this disaster it is possible to say with the most desperate sincerity and conviction that it is we who are on the way to winning the war, our army which is on the road to victory, and our industry which is on the way to creating the situation in which the defeat of Bilbao will be wiped out as surely as the defeats of Oropesa, and Talavera – so dreadful, so 'decisive' when they happened – were wiped out by Guadalajara.

When the enemy were at the gates of Madrid, and every 'expert', from the British Embassy to Long Acre, thought Madrid was done for, the Communist Party's slogan was 'He who does not believe in victory is a coward.' There were people who thought they were 'whistling in the dark'. Where are they now?

We said then that Madrid would hold because we knew the facts of Madrid and its possibilities. For the same reason we say now that despite Bilbao we are going to win the war and anyone who thinks differently is either a deliberate defeatist or ignorant of the facts of the situation.

The thing to do is to understand why Bilbao fell. Then we can understand both the extent of and the significance of that tragedy.

Reason number one is summed up in the ugly words 'non-intervention'. What smashed the defences of Bilbao? Aeroplanes and guns. Where did the aeroplanes and guns come from? From Germany and Italy. How did they get in?

They were brought in while Mr Eden was assuring the League of Nations that non-intervention was functioning nicely. They were brought in because the democratic governments let them in. They were brought in while the Second International was waiting to see 'how the new control would work'.

Why was it impossible for the Spaniards to stop them? Because the co-operation of the German and Italian fleets in the control scheme made it impossible for the Spanish fleet to operate effectively at sea, and because the farce of the so-called control reaches its peak in the fact that there is no control whatever of aeroplanes coming into the country.

Alvarez del Vayo, in a statement at Albacete on Sunday afternoon, said, 'This has exposed once more the farce of the control. I can say definitely that in the last three weeks three times as many German and Italian aeroplanes have arrived at the Bilbao front as in the three previous months.

'In the last ten days a new type of German plane, with a speed of 500 kilometres an hour, has made its appearance on this front.'

That is reason number one. Reason number two is of a different character. The question is, and it is a natural one: why were the German and Italian aeroplanes so effective on the Bilbao front, and does not their success prove that they can repeat the same thing elsewhere?

Actually the supposition is nonsense. The answer to it is Spanish geography. The fact about the situation at Bilbao is that if you have a force operating from an extensive territory and another force trying to defend a small mountainous territory with very limited possible airfields the attacking forces will almost certainly win. The defenders may theoretically have at their disposal a large fleet of aeroplanes.

Theoretically, aeroplanes can be sent in to them from elsewhere but if the aerodrome sites are sufficiently limited by the size of the territory and its mountainous character, then it is a military certainty that the majority of the aeroplanes thus sent in are being sent to be virtually massacred on the ground located and attacked by enemy raiders and bombed out of action before they can even take the air.

I do not mean to say that it is impossible to operate planes at all under such conditions, but the dice are terribly weighted against them, and unless you have virtually unlimited planes to throw away on such a defence the command of the air is impossible.

That is the simple reason why the Germans have commanded the air in the Basque country. For even given the huge number of aeroplanes that they have they would not have had sufficient command of the air to conduct the attacks they did against the infantry lines if there had been even a very much weaker government force in a position to operate in suitable air fields.

It was the misfortune of war that in Bilbao geography favoured the enemy. It was the fortune of fascist diplomacy that the Fascist powers were permitted and assisted to exploit to the full that geographical accident by the other western governments and by the fatal inaction of the Second International.

If ever an answer were needed to the speeches of the delegates who discussed the control at the Second International Congress in London in March, if ever a proof were needed, after Almería, of the terrible urgency of united action along the lines proposed by the Communist International, Bilbao is it.

The tragedy is that thousands of men should pay with their lives for the fact that we have not yet been able to get rid of Mr Bevin and his like who had those lives in their hands and gave them over to the slaughter.

The conditions of the fall of Bilbao are therefore special conditions. It would be silly to underestimate the importance of the loss. It would be just as silly to fall into the mistake of imagining that those conditions are repeated elsewhere. They are not.

It is necessary to be precise. Look at the map. Look at the lines of the front. Here is a quotation from a document used by the general staff more than ten days before Bilbao fell:

'If the Northern front were – like the Aragon front or the Mancha front or the Andalusian front – a prolongation of the central front, Bilbao would have not been in any danger despite the elements massed to take it.

'But, as is known, the Asturias, Santander and the Basque country form an isolated block which has to defend itself by its own means.

'Apart from aviation – and the lack of aerodromes heavily reduced the value of this weapon to us – it is impossible to send overland any assistance to the Basques, the Asturians and the people of Santander, and the overseas route is hopeless above all, because of the presence in the Mediterranean of the German and Italian fleets.'

It is worth repeating that that was written nearly a fortnight ago and therefore cannot be regarded as an attempt in any sense to excuse the fall of Bilbao.

There is a third reason for the loss of Bilbao. Everyone knows it. It is that during the period of the Caballero government, the government was either incapable or unwilling to put the military and economic machinery of the country into a state wherein it would be possible effectively to do the only thing which could have saved Bilbao, namely, to conduct a series of real, effective offensives on other fronts.

We know how long the Communist Party fought to get the government to establish a regular army at all. We know how after Málaga, although compulsory mobilisation existed on paper the government was incapable of putting it into effect.

We know what happened in Catalonia and what the Caballero government did in that situation. That, too, like the geographical factor, was something special. The Caballero government has gone, and with it has been swept away the principal obstacle to the organisation of the overwhelming manpower of Republican Spain.

And now the military forces, backed by sufficient reserve, supplied by high-production war industry, with the aid of the united action of the anti-fascists of the world, will, before many months, set the radios of Berlin and Rome singing a different tune.

It is a demonstrable fact that the human and economic resources of the People's Front are overwhelming. Already Pasionaria said yesterday, 'We have scores of thousands of men who compare favourably as soldiers with the men of any army in Europe.'

We are in sight of an army which will be one of the most powerful in the west of Europe, we are in sight of a self-sufficient war industry, and it seems – and it is no less vital than the other factors – that we are at long last in sight of united action by the Internationals.

Daily Worker, 25 June 1937

NAZI WAR-FLEET TO REMAIN OFF SPAIN

Reported Italian Landing At Málaga

VALENCIA, Thursday.

In the face of German and Italian aggression and British government cowardice, Spain stands ready today to defend itself with all the forces at its command.

We are informed here that the Foreign Office has given directions to the British press to 'play down' the gravity of the situation. I know also from my own information that several weeks ago a meeting of heads of news agencies and of newspapers was held first in New York, and later in London, at which also it was decided to agree to 'play down' the gravity of events.

On the fronts here when an officer declares that the enemy are not advancing in force, when they are advancing in force, he is shot as a traitor. It seems that in England the reward for that sort of thing is another spell of Cabinet office.

Because of this ugly conspiracy of silence and confusion, it is necessary to face very clearly the situation as it really is in the Mediterranean.

Ten days ago I reported that peace in the Mediterranean was hanging by a thread. The thread is fraying fast. If you do not act it will break.

The position is this: The German and Italian fleets, after their governments had failed to secure the immediate joint bombardment by the French, British, German and Italian fleets of Spanish ports, and seizure of Spanish submarines, are getting ready to take Spanish merchant ships and possibly ships of war, too.

It may be that three or four months ago the Republic would have had to swallow this in the way it had to swallow the bombing of Madrid by German aeroplanes with German pilots. That was an open act of war against the Republic.

The Republic, partly because it was militarily weak, partly

because it still hoped that the other democracies of western Europe would act in accordance with international law, and with the most elementary principles of self-defence, did not treat the attack as an act of war by the German government.

A lot of water has flown under the bridges since then. Today the Republic is strong. Today the Republic knows what to think of the policy of the wretched Eden.

The Republic – and it is necessary that the world should understand the fact – is not going to stand for more nonsense. Aggression will meet with the punishment it deserves. The Republic today has a better army and a better navy than Spain has had since before the Spanish-American war, at the turn of the century.

The Republic is determined to win this war. If the British Labour Party allows the British government to continue the policy of encouragement to Germany and Italy, which induces Germany and Italy to lay violent hands on the Republic, the Republic will answer for itself: but who will then answer for the peace of the world?

The Republic can make no further concessions. Nobody could dare to ask it to make them. If the German and Italian aggression is permitted to go to those lengths, then the responsibility for what happens next will lie on the shoulders, first, of the British government; secondly, on those of Mr Bevin, Mr Citrine, Mr Gillies and all those so-called British labour leaders – although they represent neither the interests of Britain nor the interests of labour – who have sought and are still seeking to prevent united action of the two Internationals on behalf of Spain, and on behalf of the peace of the world.

Do not believe a word of it when people tell you there is a lessening of tension in the Mediterranean. There is nothing of the kind. They told you that before Almería and after Almería. They told you that before the German news bureau invented the Leipzig torpedoes three days after the official German radio station at Stuttgart denied their existence.

Chapter Five

DEFEAT AND THE WIDER CRISIS

Cockburn left Spain in the summer of 1937, and only returned again during the civil war for a short visit to Madrid in the autumn of that year. He continued to follow the crisis in the diplomatic sphere, as it became increasingly integrated with the wider struggle to stop the aggressive expansionist policy of the Axis powers. Included here are his despatches from the League of Nations.

Daily Worker, 13 September 1937

EDEN BAULKED IN PLAN TO AID FRANCO

Dramatic Story Of Struggle For Anti-Piracy Pact

After about thirty hours of tough diplomatic wrestling with absolutely no holds barred there emerged late yesterday from the Social Hall of Nyon* a plan for dealing with piracy in the Mediterranean, of which it is possible to say this:

1) It is a considerably, indeed essentially different document from the monstrous affair which Anthony Eden tried to eyewash the delegates into accepting on Friday afternoon and which British propagandists late that evening were trying to foist on the world as a plan to which everyone had agreed.

2) The plot to get belligerent rights for Franco which would have come off if the first British proposals had got through has, for the time being, been dropped by the stout and unshakeable

* (Nyon, near Geneva, was the venue for a conference called to prevent attacks on neutral ships in the Mediterranean.

resistance of the Soviet delegation, which is backed by at least one other power.

3) Despite the negative advantages, the plan remains so flabby an affair that delegations variously interested in carrying out the work they were sent to Nyon to do have had to insist on referring the plan back to their governments on the grounds that the invitation to Nyon was an invitation to work out means of putting a stop to piracy in the Mediterranean and the plan actually worked out seems scarcely to conform with the terms of that invitation.

4) The plan – with all its improvements over the original one – contains all the defects which must be present in any scheme built up on the shaky foundation of a state of affairs in which the fact that the Italian and German governments are making war on the Spanish government remains unrecognised.

5) Within these limits the fight put up against the original plan with its absurd 'Zoning' system – now wiped off the map after about twelve hours of public existence – has resulted in the British and French being forced publicly to recognise at least the letter of their collective responsibility for action against Fascist piracy.

Here is the roundabout story of the diplomatic struggle out of which the present plan emerged. When just after 5.30 on Friday evening the Nyon conference went into private session, the British plot for the so-called Anglo-French plan showed immediately that they had every hope of forcing the plan through at such a pace that the delegates would have signed it almost before they knew what was in it.

For one thing, the British were the only people who had their naval experts on the spot. For another thing, it seems they had 'forgotten' to have any copies of the plan made.

So Eden – rather in the manner of a director of a speculative company who is not too anxious to have the shareholders studying closely the directors' report, proceeded to read it from the only available copy, pausing briefly after each paragraph to allow the Chairman to say, 'I suppose we may take it everyone agrees to that?' and then hurrying on to the next paragraph.

After mumbling through two or three paragraphs in this manner he came to the crucial clause stating that submarines must not torpedo ships without first conforming to the London Naval Treaty of 1930 and the protocol of 1936 on the humanisation of submarine warfare.

The essence of this is the provision that a submarine must not torpedo a ship without first having assured the safety of the crew.

Concealed in the attempt to include this apparently innocent and even humane provision in the agreement were the following two points:

The protocol and the treaty are for application in time of war. Their provisions are applicable to belligerents.

If such a clause was inserted without qualification into the Nyon Agreement that would have, in fact, been an immediate recognition of belligerent rights for Franco.

Secondly, it would have amounted, of course, to an invitation to submarines to sink Spanish ships, provided they did so in accordance with the rules.

This, therefore, was for the British the crucial point, and it was on this point that the defenders of peace against Fascism swung into action.

Eden was faced with a straightforward demand by other delegates that the clause referring to the London Treaty and the protocol should be omitted, thus condemning the sinking of pirate submarines regardless of whether or not they observed these rules.

This forced Eden to show his hand. In view of the fact that the whole purpose of inserting the reference to the Lodon protocol in the Agreement was to open the door to belligerent rights, he had to state that he could not possibly accept the elimination of that clause.

For another hour the trouble went on behind closed doors and the meeting came to an end without agreement.

Daily Worker, 22 November 1937

CABINET PLANS BLOW AT SPAIN

Will Withdraw The Ambassador

A new and particularly scandalous move in the betrayal of the Spanish Republic and the recognition of the Fascist General Franco is being secretly planned in the Foreign Office.

It is proposed to withdraw the Ambassador at present accredited to the Republic, leave a Chargé d'Affaires as the highest ranking British diplomatic representative with the Republic, and thus create an equality of diplomatic status between the Chargé d'Affaires in Barcelona and the chief British agent just appointed to Salamanca.

The present British Ambassador to Spain is Sir Henry Chilton. Although he is only sixty years old and has shown no particular signs of decay, it is proposed sometime within the next two or three weeks, to withdraw him on the grounds either of old age or ill health – or possibly it will suddenly be discovered that he has urgent private reasons for coming to England.

No successor will be appointed, and thus the 'equalisation' of the status of the diplomatic missions to the Republic and to the Fascist invaders will be stealthily accomplished.

The move is apparently designed to be particularly offensive to the French government, which has recently sacked its former Ambassador – Herbette – who functioned at Hendaye and was well known to be in the closest cahoots with the Fascists, and has instead sent a new Ambassador to Barcelona itself.

Sir Henry Chilton has also been carrying on his diplomatic duties from the safety and comfort of Hendaye, instead of from the Embassy first at Madrid, then at Valencia and now at Barcelona.

He is a strong monarchist, who has made no secret of his profound sympathy, not with the government to which he is accredited, but with the rebellious Generals who have called in the Italian, German and Moorish invaders to overthrow that government and establish a Fascist occupation.

I understand that Sir Henry Chilton on one occasion actually gave a written recommendation to the Military Governor of Irún, stating that he was a fit and proper person to look after the Basque children whom it was then proposed to repatriate. The Military Governor of Irún was none other than the terrorist ruffian Troncoso, now fortunately under lock and key in a French jail.

The fact that the British Ambassador accredited to the Republic has never been in Spain since the war began, and has used his position at Hendaye on the frontier of Fascist Spain as a means of keping in close touch with the Fascists is scandalous enough.

Not less so is the fact that Mr Leche, the present British

Chargé d'Affaires in Republican Spain, is also a strong and open sympathiser with the enemies of the Republic.

Now, instead of appointing a proper Ambassador – like the French – to the Republic, the Ambassador is to be withdrawn altogether, even from Hendaye, and Mr Leche left as the highest ranking British diplomat on the government side.

Daily Worker, 11 May 1938

BRITISH PLANS GO ALL AWRY AT THE LEAGUE

GENEVA, Tuesday.

Three times within the past few hours Alvarez del Vayo has had to send a special courier from his hotel to the League building to collect the great basketfuls of telegrams and letters of support pouring in from all parts of the world.

The majority, I am told, are from Britain.

From them, Vayo, as he prepares his statement on the Spanish case for the League, has a vivid picture of the real mass of England, so grossly misrepresented here by Lord Halifax.

The day has been full of jolts for Lord Halifax, who now openly takes the position here of Commander-in-Chief of the pro-Fascist forces.

The whole British idea was to rush through the agenda of this Council at breakneck speed in order to give as little opportunity as possible for public opinion in Britain to rouse itself to what is happening.

Already they are going about lamenting openly that everything is taking just three times as long to get through as they have planned.

First, as I have asserted yesterday, Vayo flatly rejected the Halifax plan to rush him into speaking today, immediately after Halifax himself.

Then Lord Halifax's own speech on the Anglo-Italian Agreement, which was intended as a big show for Chamberlain, was punctured and deflated by Litvinov in a little spech as neat as a lighted cigarette pressed to a balloon.

Lord Halifax had been bleating about 'the contribution to peace' represented by the Anglo-Italian Pact.

The French were reserved. The Belgians were coolly non-committal.

Then Litvinov, in his chilliest manner, remarked:

'My government, which takes particularly to heart everything which relates to international peace, quite naturally welcomes any agreement reached between various countries removing the misunderstandings and disputes existing between them.

'But in dealing with bilateral pacts, we have to take into consideration not only their effect upon the relationship between the two parties concerned, but also upon the relations between those parties and the rest of the world.

'We have also to take into consideration the effect which such agreements will have on those problems which are still before the League of Nations, and which still remain to be dealt with.

'We therefore reserve our final judgment upon the importance of this agreement from this point of view.'

After that came the speech of Wellington Koo, representing China, in which he outlined the wrongs done to China, with special emphasis on the Japanese use of poison-gas, and suggested the invocation of Article 17 of the Covenant of the League, which would automatically involve the coming into play of the Sanctions Article.

There seems to be some possibility that the Chinese may now compel the calling of the Assembly to consider the question.

It had been fixed that the Abyssinians were to appear at a Council meeting this afternoon. At the last moment it turned out that the British were proposing to have Lord Halifax suddenly presenting the Abyssinians at this meeting a string of British arguments.

The Abyssinians then, having refused to go into such a meeting, insisted that they must have a chance to study the British arguments in advance.

They have adjourned the meeting probably until Thursday, and it now seems likely that the Emperor in person may after all attend.

Daily Worker, 12 May 1938

SPAIN CONDEMNS BRITISH GUILT: LEAGUE SENSATION

GENEVA, Wednesday.
The Chamberlain-Halifax government received at Geneva today the biggest 'dressing down' it has received for years in an international gathering.

It got it in the speech before the Council of the League of Alvarez del Vayo, representing the Spanish government.

The scene was sensational.

As del Vayo spoke, developing his denunciation of the German-Italian aggression, and of the part played in it increasingly by the Chamberlain government, Lord Halifax sat with his face covered in his hands, occasionally removing them and scribbling agitated notes to the other members of the Council whenever a particularly unsavoury point on British policy was made.

The debate was adjourned after a sensational attempt by Lord Halifax to close it without permitting del Vayo to reply to the British government observations.

Vayo had spoken and flatly accused the British government of aiding and abetting the Fascist powers.

Halifax, in a speech 'good enough to bury him with', as someone remarked, made an effort to reply. His observations were of so monstrous a character that even the most hard-boiled 'old Geneva hands' were shocked.

The New Zealand delegate then spoke, giving the fullest support of the New Zealand government to the demands of Spain. Litvinov also declared the full support of the Soviet Union.

It was after that that they attempted to close the session. Vayo rose and demanded to reply. They attempted to force him to reply immediately or not at all.

Vayo answered, 'We are dealing with matters of the utmost gravity, and I had supposed that the representative of Spain would have at least been given the opportunity to study calmly the observations made here.'

The Council finally agreed to adjourn the session and to admit that Vayo is to speak again later.

'It is both strange and saddening,' said del Vayo, in his speech, 'to observe to what extent the language of those who claim to be defenders of the Geneva institution becomes identical with that of its enemies.

'It is no less extraordinary that the policy of misrepresentation and sabotage, designed to destroy the League of Nations, a policy employed with growing success since 1935 by Berlin and Rome, should in other capitals attack the most irresponsible, or perhaps the most responsible and urgent collaborators.

'We have watched day by day this incomprehensible desertion of certain democracies.

'We have watched them conspire with the aggressors, and sign agreements with them which legalise intervention.

'These democracies have brought nearer the day when their own cities will fall victim to the same atrocities as have filled my country with horror and death.

'But none of these circumstances have been able to disturb the composure with which the Spanish government is defending, internally and externally, the interests of its people.

'It has been suggested that Spain could best have contributed to world peace by ceasing to exist as an independent nation before the May session.

'Our international courtesy, I regret to say, does not go as far as that.

'Those who base their foreign policy on the speedy demise of the Spanish people are destined to suffer the same disillusionment as those who believed that the signing of certain 'realistic' agreements would coincide with the 'reality' of the entry of the Italian divisions into Barcelona.

'The Spanish government suggests that investigations should be made into the despatch of Italian reinforcements, outside of men, during the course of the negotiations which took place between the governments of Italy and the United Kingdom.

'Non-intervention has been a complete and utter failure. The fact is obvious to the naked eye and, moreover, has confirmation in the Anglo-Italian Agreement of 16 April.

'In this agreement the British government expounded a hypothesis according to which Italian troops and materials now in Spain may remain there until the end of the war.

'The existence of such a hypothesis logically implies that the outcome of the war can be decided by the active and direct intervention of those Italian troops and armaments.

'Non-intervention is an instrument through which the Spanish conflict may be finally decided by the intervention of Germany and Italy.

'Non-intervention is the policy in regard to Spain which harmonises with a policy of rapprochement with European totalitarian states. This policy inevitably leads to war.

'What the Spanish government claims is the simple re-establishment of the ordinary rules of international law, that is, that its right to buy war material should be restored.'

Daily Worker, 14 May 1938

SPAIN CHALLENGES HALIFAX ON ARMS EMBARGO

Chamberlain In Dock Before The World

GENEVA, Friday.

The Spanish government today shattered with the force of a political bombshell the complacency of the pro-Fascist powers under the generalship of Lord Halifax in the Council of the League of Nations.

For two hours, between the democrats and Lord Halifax has been going on a battle of a violence seldom seen at the League of Nations. The British delegation is in panic.

Taking them entirely by surprise, del Vayo came to the Council Chamber and demanded:

First, that Lord Halifax should answer 'Yes' or 'No' to one of two definite questions which the world has been asking for months to the Chamberlain government.

Second, the Council shall declare by public vote whether it will not 'envisage' immediate end of non-intervention, or whether instead its members will dare publicly to go back upon the solemn pledge on the subject of non-intervention for which all but two of them voted not longer ago than 2 October of last year.

Third, that when Lord Halifax talked on intervention 'on both sides' he should be aware of the fact that on the government's side there are a number of volunteers, not exceeding 6,000, while on the other side there are at least 100,000 men of the Italian army.

Fourth, that if Lord Halifax does not believe this he should agree to put the matter to the test by having the League investigate.

'If they force Lord Halifax to vote on this, there is scarcely a seat for Chamberlain in England,' declared one of the cleverest of foreign observers, over del Vayo's speech today.

The exposure of Lord Halifax was dramatically completed. First as regards the resolution proposed by the Spanish government. This resolution had recalled that on October last thirty-two states, including all members of the Council except Bolivia and Peru, voted in favour of a resolution declaring that unless 'in the near future' foreign troops were withdrawn from Spain the members of the League who are members of the Non-Intervention Committee would consider withdrawing from it.

The Spanish government's resolution today expressed hope that these governments did not consider that expression 'in the near future' covered a period of seven months. The Spanish government now 'invites the member states of the League who voted in favour of the draft resolution of 2 October to envisage, as from the present moment the end of the policy of non-intervention'.

Lord Halifax, taken entirely by surprise, in a lame speech declared himself 'absolutely opposed' to the resolution put forward by the Spanish government.

This, if it means anything, means that Lord Halifax is now entirely opposed to the withdrawal of foreign troops from Spain.

He had been faced with this definite question from del Vayo. 'If, irrespective of the Anglo-Italian Agreement, Italy and Germany continue the intervention in Spain, in the name of what morality and justice can you go on depriving the legal Spanish government of its rights in international law?

'If my question receives no satisfactory answer, no one will be surprised if the conduct of the two powers who initiated the Non-intervention Agreement and are still defending it, should appear monstrous and inexplicable to the Spanish people and that they should only see in it a deliberate attempt to defeat their struggle for independence and to deliver them into the hands of the foreign invaders.

This question Lord Halifax failed to answer as he failed to answer another. He had said in an earlier speech that he deplored the sufferings in Spain which he described as 'inseparable' from modern warfare.

Speaking with great emphasis del Vayo said he could not allow such a statement by Lord Halifax to pass without a special comment. He accused Lord Halifax of using words which might justifiably be interpreted as a defence for the bombardments of Guernica, Almería and Barcelona.

'I should like to express the hope that these words of the representative of the United Kingdom do not in any way weaken the assurance of the British government to the resolution of the Council of 29 May, 1937, expressing emotion at the "horrors resulting from the use of certain methods of warfare" and condemning the "employment in the Spanish struggle of methods contrary to international law and the bombing of open towns" '.

Strongly supporting the fight of del Vayo came M. Litvinov, representative of the Soviet Union, who spoke out while the rest remained silent.

So persistent were they that the Council will have to meet again late tonight to continue discussion.